# OFFSHORE

*BRITAIN AND THE*
*EUROPEAN IDEA*

# OFFSHORE

## BRITAIN AND THE EUROPEAN IDEA

## Giles Radice

I.B.Tauris & Co Ltd
*Publishers*
London · New York

Published in 1992 by
I.B.Tauris & Co Ltd
45 Bloomsbury Square
London WC1A 2HY

175 Fifth Avenue
New York
NY 10010

In the United States of America
and Canada distributed by
St Martin's Press
175 Fifth Avenue
New York
NY 10010

The publishers wish to thank the following for permission to
reproduce cartoons and the supply of photographic prints: p.9 top:
*The Evening Standard*/Solo Syndication; bottom: *Private Eye*;
p.111 top: Archiv fur Kunst und Geschichte, Berlin; bottom: The
Mansell Collection, London; pp.112 and 113: *Punch*; p.114 top:
*The Evening Standard*/Solo Syndication and the Centre for the
Study of Cartoons and Caricature, University of Kent at
Canterbury; bottom: the *Daily Mail*/Solo Syndication and the
Centre for the Study of Cartoons and Caricature, University of
Kent at Canterbury; p.115: *The Economist*; p.116: *The Spectator*;
p.117 Lurie, Cartoonews, Inc., NYC, USA. Every effort has been
made to trace the original sources of the cartoons; if any have been
omitted or are incorrect, the publishers will correct these
acknowledgements in any further editions of the book, provided
they are informed.

A CIP record for this book is available from the British Library

Library of Congress catalog card number: 91-68024
A full CIP record is available from the Library of Congress

ISBN 1-85043-362-3

ISBN (USA only) 1-85043-529-4

Printed and bound in Great Britain by
WBC Limited, Bridgend, Mid Glamorgan.

# Contents

# List of Cartoons

vi

# Preface

This book, which is an exploration by a convinced European of Britain's long, complex and often tortuous relationship with the Continent, inevitably relies heavily on the work and help of others. I am extremely grateful to Professor Richard Evans, Peter Hennessy, Professor Keith Robbins and Professor Conrad Russell for their historical advice. Julian Barnes, Annette Morgan, Elinor Sinclair and Axel Queval have kindly assisted me on French attitudes. I would like to thank Anthony Glees, Peter Schulze, Angelika Volle, and my many German friends at successive Königswinter conferences for giving me an insight into German attitudes. Robert Worcester of MORI, the EC London Information Office and the *Eurobarometer* office in Brussels have provided me with invaluable opinion survey material on British attitudes. Sixth formers at Park View School, Chester-le-Street, and Roseberry Comprehensive School, Pelton, in my North Durham constituency were kind enough to respond to my questions on their views on Britain and Europe.

I am indebted to Helen Wallace and William Wallace for their profound knowledge of the European Community. I am grateful to Rt Hon. John Biffen MP, Rt

Hon. Edward Heath MP, Rt Hon. Sir Geoffrey Howe MP, Lord Jenkins of Hillhead, David Lea and Rt Hon. Peter Shore MP for allowing me to interview them on European matters. Charles Clarke, John Eatwell, Rt Hon. Gerald Kaufman MP, George Robertson MP and David Ward have all added to my knowledge of the Labour party's change of position on the EC. Clarissa and Rosemary White have given me valuable help on literary allusions. My thanks to the House of Commons Library for their customary efficient service.

Penny Cooper, Professor Richard Evans, Peter Hennessy, Professor Keith Robbins, Lisanne Radice and Helen Wallace have commented on drafts of the book. I am grateful to Iradj Bagherzade and Lisanne Radice for helpful editorial advice, and to Emma Sinclair-Webb for her support. I would like to give special thanks to Penny Cooper for her exceptional research work and Gillian Jacomb-Hood for her patience in interpreting my handwriting and for her skill with the word processor. I take full responsibility for the views expressed in the book.

# Introduction

'Passengers will need landing cards, except for those holding British and European Community passports.' The Tannoy announcement, as the British Airways flight from Frankfurt began its descent to Heathrow one morning in the summer of 1990, reminded my German friend, if he needed reminding, that our 'offshore' mentality was alive and well. Despite nearly twenty years of membership of the European Community (EC), the British still feel apart, separated from the Continent not merely by a strip of water but also by a complex bundle of attitudes and prejudices. Many of us remain reluctant Europeans.

Yet, the 1990s will bring the British Isles economically, politically and psychologically closer to the mainland of Europe. The establishment of the Single European Market by the end of 1992 will reduce barriers to the free movement of people, goods, services and capital. Despite the self-defeating opt-outs from the single currency and from the social protocol negotiated for Britain by John Major at Maastricht in December 1991, the agreements on economic and monetary union and political union will greatly increase economic and political ties. In 1993, the opening of the

1

Channel Tunnel will link Britain physically with the Continent.

I attempt in this book to answer two questions. Why have the British been such reluctant Europeans? And why are British attitudes to Europe now gradually changing?

I write as a committed supporter of the European idea. I became a convert when I was eighteen. Ten years after the war, in the summer of 1955 between school and national service, I set out to bicycle from Rotterdam to Rome. As the foreign ministers of the Six prepared for the momentous Messina Conference which launched the Common Market, I pedalled furiously along the roads and lanes of Holland, Belgium, Luxemburg, Germany, France and Italy. Most nights, I stayed at youth hostels where I met my Continental contemporaries. Excitedly we discussed the hopes of building a new and better Europe in which war, whose detritus still visibly scarred the land, should be ended for ever and prosperity for all be assured. It became clear to me that not only was it right that Europeans should unite but also that Britain could not stand aside from such a constructive and imaginative project. The British had to support the idea of European unity.

I was therefore greatly disappointed when British politicians, still insistent on behaving like leaders of a world power, refused to participate in the creation of the Common Market. Even in the mid 1950s, it seemed an appallingly anachronistic decision. As a budding politician in the 1960s, I applauded both Harold Macmillan's and Harold Wilson's belated though unsuccessful attempts to take Britain into the European Community. Elected to parliament at a by-election in March 1973, I was too late to vote in the House of

Commons with the sixty-nine Labour rebel MPs for British entry in October 1971. But I recorded a 'yes' vote in the 1975 referendum when, to my relief, by more than two to one, the British decided to stay in the EC. Since then I have watched, sometimes with sadness and dismay, as successive governments struggled to come to terms with British membership. Far too often, particularly under Mrs Thatcher's governments but also under John Major at Maastricht, Britain has adopted a negative or minimalist posture. A recent survey of Britain's record in the European Community is entitled *An Awkward Partner*.[1] That is a harsh but just verdict on nearly twenty years of British membership.

However, it would be less than fair not to acknowledge that in pursuing such a cautious approach to the EC, British political leaders have, at least until the late 1980s, been broadly in line with British public opinion. The polls over the last eighteen years show that the majority of the citizens of the other member states, with the exception of Denmark, are strongly in favour of the European Community. In contrast, the British have always been sceptical. Even at the end of 1990, when, according to the EC Eurobarometer, British backing for the Community at 53 per cent was equal to the all-time high recorded in mid 1989, it was still the lowest in the EC.[2]

So my consideration of British reluctance in the first part of the book examines not only the failures of political leadership but also the geographical, historical, social and cultural factors which have helped shape hostile popular attitudes. The roots of British ambivalence about Continental Europe lie deeply embedded in the national experience, identity and self-image.

I seek not so much to judge but to explain. Being a

convinced European does not mean that I am not also a patriot who is very conscious of Britain's past. As a child I was brought up on the exploits of Drake, Nelson, Wolfe, Clive and Wellington. I was also taught to be proud of my ancestors. My paternal great-great-grand-father was an Italian nationalist, fortunate enough to be able to come to this country as a political refugee. His descendants have been British academics, teachers, business executives and civil servants (including a generation of Indian civilians – the so called 'Heaven born'). On my mother's side, I come from a long line of soldiers, MPs and JPs. My forebears on both my father's and mother's side fought – and died – for this country. Above all, I have learnt to value the contribution of Britain to world civilisation, especially its scientific and technological achievements, its magnificent literature, the creation of parliamentary democracy and the development of the welfare state.

I can understand if not sympathise with those who find it difficult to accept that Britain is now no more (and no less) than a medium-sized European power. Even during my own lifetime, I have seen a dramatic shift. When I was a child in India during the last days of the British Raj, I used to gaze up at the map of the world, a quarter of which was coloured in red. Now in the 1990s, we have shrunk back to being a small but relatively prosperous group of offshore islands, close to the mainland of Europe.

It is this change which makes it inevitable that Britain's future should lie in Europe. We may still have world interests; we may still have an affinity with the United States; but our main priority must be to build our relationship with our European neighbours. We are linked historically and culturally to the Continent. We now also have strong economic, political and strategic ties. Above all, we are beginning to understand that it is in our interests to combine with other European countries in those spheres where Britain can no longer act effectively alone. At a time when the collapse of the Soviet Empire has led to change, disruption and even disintegration in Central and Eastern Europe and especially in the former Soviet Union itself, it is all the more essential that the EC increases its influence and strength. The form that closer European union will take will be *sui generis*: in some respects, it will be confederal, in others federal. But the direction will – and should – be towards greater unity. We have to be part of the process of European integration. Britain must embrace the European idea.

There is now a substantial and growing body of British opinion which accepts this inescapable conclusion.[3] The majority now favour stronger ties with other members of the EC. The British now feel closer to the Continentals than they do to the Americans or the Commonwealth. Above all, they do not wish to be left out of European developments.

The second part of the book examines the forces which are now pulling the British towards the mainland of Europe. Already the impact of industry and trade has linked the British economy closer to the Continent; 1992 will strengthen the process of integration. The combination of travel, education, employment and increasing access to Continental goods, services, cuisine and cultures is making a growing number of the British, particularly the younger generation, feel more European.[4] The development of a social and regional dimension is making the EC more attractive. And the political, business, trade union and local authority establishments are becoming more accustomed to operating within a European context.

My conclusion is that, though the British have thought themselves a race apart and, to a considerable extent, still do, attitudes are now changing. Over the next decade, the British, even under the Conservatives, will become more and more European. It is all the more essential that the re-elected Major government develops a more positive agenda during its Presidency of the European Council from July to December 1992 and over the next five years, and that the Labour opposition sustains its new commitment to the European Community.

# PART I

# Reluctant Europeans

**Above:** Low's famous 1940 cartoon, titled 'Very well, alone', symbolizes the defiant patriotism which kept out Hitler.

**Left:** 'I hate frogs.' The *Private eye* cartoon of December 1991 highlights the unacceptable face of English nationalism: contempt for foreigners.

*"A xenophobic bigot? I prefer the term 'Eurosceptic'"*

# – 1 –

# 'A Thousand Years
of History'

There is a fine Low cartoon of 1940 in which a British Tommy, feet planted firmly on island soil, shakes his fist defiantly in the direction of the Continent, and shouts across the waves: 'Very well, alone'.[1] Our strong sense of national pride, our 'off-shore' mentality, our attitude to the European Com munity have all been shaped by such powerfully nostalgic images as this. Too often since the war we have allowed ourselves to become prisoners of our own past.

Consider these two examples of 'romantic chauvinism', occasions when a notable pair of political leaders indulged in shameless sentimentality about British history.[2] In October 1962, in his highly emotional speech to his party conference in Brighton, Hugh Gaitskell, then leader of the Labour Party, turned to history to justify his rejection of British membership of the Common Market on the terms negotiated by the Conservative government. Accusing the Tories of selling the Commonwealth 'down the river', he cited the military help received from the old Dominions at the First World War battles of Vimy Ridge and Gallipoli. He reminded his party that 'there have been evil features in European

11

history . . . it has its two faces and we do not know as yet which is the one which will dominate'. Arguing that the founders of the EC openly sought a federal state, Gaitskell warned apocalyptically but inaccurately that it would mean 'the end of Britain as an independent nation state, the end of a thousand years of history'.[3]

Nearly thirty years later, Margaret Thatcher, facing what she perceived as the threat to national sovereignty coming from the EC, also embraced the historical tendency. In the last two years of her premiership, she peppered her speeches with references to the Magna Carta of 1215, to the 'Glorious Revolution of 1688', and to Britain's ancient parliamentary and legal traditions. In an interview in March 1990 in *Der Spiegel*, she erroneously boasted to a German audience: 'We have the oldest parliament in Europe – it's 700 years old. We are not easily dominated . . . people should not forget what history teaches us'.[4]

Then, following her October 1990 statement to the Commons on the Rome Summit, she rounded dramatically on her parliamentary opponents with a blaze of historical gunfire. Britain would trade better with 'the great history behind sterling' than it would with a single currency, she told a Tory critic. European economic and monetary union would undermine the sovereignty of parliament which had 'served this country and the rest of the world very well', she assured the House. She continued: 'It is one thing to have a United States of America from a newly settled country, but it is a different thing for ancient nation states, each with its own traditions'. She concluded that 'the way to balance out the different views of Europe, as we have traditionally done throughout history, is by retaining our national identity.' For Margaret Thatcher, as for Hugh

Gaitskell, greater European involvement for Britain spelled the end of a thousand years of history.

Certainly Britain has a unique historical experience. Its system of laws, its parliament, its constitutional development, set the nation apart from mainland Europe. Britain pioneered the Industrial Revolution. With control of the seas, it became the first world empire, ruling at least a quarter of the globe. In 1940, it stood alone against Hitler. It came through two world wars as one of the victor nations. Unlike the other eleven members of the European Community, Britain has not experienced serious military defeat, occupation, civil war, or revolution for at least two hundred years. Listen to Enoch Powell, fervent English nationalist, boasting about past British achievements:

> Compare the story of Britain in the 20th century with that of her supposedly successful competitors, France or Germany or Japan. They made a ghastly hash of their countries, alongside which Britain, whether due to the qualities of her people and institutions or to her insular character or more likely to the combination of both, came relatively unscathed through immense transitions and vicissitudes.[5]

Splendid stuff but how relevant is it to the 1990s?

History is crucial to an understanding not only of our own traditions but also those of other nations. But it is wise to be extremely cautious when politicians quote from history to lend authority to their own insular prescriptions. If a study of the past helps put the present into perspective, it is not always much of a guide to the future.

When in December 1962 the former American secretary of state, Dean Acheson, delivered his harsh verdict that 'Great Britain has lost an empire and has not yet found a role', he was warning the British against the seductive charms of their history. His sub-text was that Britain should now accept its destiny as a medium-sized European nation and that, in playing this new European role, lessons of history derived from its past were more of a hindrance than a help. Dean Acheson's advice remains as valid as on the day it was delivered.

## A Tudor Legacy

The English nationalism, to which Hugh Gaitskell and Margaret Thatcher were appealing, goes back to the Tudor period. Central to its development was the establishment of a national church, the dominance of English culture, the triumph of common law and, above all, parliamentary sovereignty.

England, though of course, not Britain or the British Isles, was united in the eleventh century, before other European states. But historians argue about the extent to which it is possible to identify much of a sense of English national identity before the beginning of the fourteenth century, and even in the fifteenth century there was no conception of England as a unitary state. The Reformation was the turning point. Henry VIII's break with Rome over his ruthless determination to divorce Catherine of Aragon and marry Anne Boleyn led to the creation by the end of the 1530s of an autonomous 'Anglican' church, with the sovereign at its head. The rapid spread of Protestant ideas over the next twenty years, the publication of Cranmer's English Prayer Book, the translation of the Bible, services conducted in the vernacular, the dependence of English Catholics on foreign support – all these combined not only to associate the Anglican church with national independence but to build a new national state. In his polemical Protestant tract, the 'Book of Martyrs', published in 1560 and ordered by Elizabeth to be placed alongside the Bible in every church, John Foxe referred to England as an 'elect nation' under a godly queen, singled out by God as an instrument of divine providence.

Vital to the development of English nationhood was the supremacy of English culture. By the middle of the fourteenth century English had replaced Norman French in the law courts, and the opening of parliament was conducted for the first time in English. But it was during the reign of Elizabeth that English became the predominant medium of communication for the nobility and gentry throughout England, Wales and Ireland.[6] When at Tilbury in 1588 the Queen appealed in English to her subjects to resist the Spanish Armada, she was speaking in the language of patriotism and national unity: 'I know I have the body but of a weak and feeble woman, but I have the heart and stomach of a king, and of a King of England too'. In Shakespeare's hands emerged a new nationalist vision of England as a 'scepter'd isle' and 'other Eden', a 'precious stone set in the silver sea'.

The Tudor period also saw the triumph of English common law, the customary law of England as unified and developed by itinerant royal justices from the twelfth century onwards. As a consequence of the break with Rome, the church's jurisdictional immunity was removed in the 1530s, while under Elizabeth the Welsh and Irish were only granted the rights of the freeborn

English if they accepted the English common law. The dominance of common law and common lawyers like Sir Edward Coke, Elizabeth and James I's attorney general, gave England a distinctive system of remedy and precedent, in contrast to continental civil law systems based on written legal codes setting out positive rights and duties.

Parliament had an important role in the Tudor polity. Medieval monarchs had summoned parliaments when they required money to pay for their wars. Under the Tudors, Henry VIII and Elizabeth needed the support of the political class for their religious settlements. The Henrican and Elizabethan parliaments established not only that parliamentary consent was required for new legislation and new taxes but also, crucially, that the crown in parliament was sovereign, in the sense that it could make laws that bound church and state.

The civil wars of the 1640s, as a consequence of which the Stuart king, Charles I, lost his head, were in part a struggle between crown and parliament for supremacy. The 'Glorious Revolution' of 1688, which established William and Mary jointly on the throne in place of James II, confirmed the victory of parliament over the crown. During the eighteenth and nineteenth centuries, parliament not only became dominant but also, through the gradual extension of the franchise, more representative of the nation.

At the end of the nineteenth century, the constitutional theorist, A. V. Dicey, was expounding in his *Law of the Constitution* the doctrine of exclusive parliamentary sovereignty, whereby there was no limitation on the powers of parliament. Only parliament had the right to make or unmake laws and no person or body had the right to override or set aside parliamentary legislation. He also pointed out that, unlike other democratic constitutions, the British constitution was based on convention rather than on a written statement of principle. The 1688 settlement may have upheld the concept that monarchs were not above the law, but neither in 1688 nor subsequently in 1707, when England and Scotland were united by the Act of Union, was a formal constitution on the later Continental model adopted.[7] In many ways the British constitution is an old-fashioned construct, derived from the Tudors.

Notice how all these symbols of nationalism – the Anglican church, parliamentary sovereignty, the distinctive legal and constitutional systems and, of course, the English language – are English (not British) in origin. The English are too often inclined to forget that there are three other nations in the British Isles. Wales was incorporated by conquest in the thirteenth century and formally merged by the 1536 Act of Union. Yet the Welsh remain culturally distinct, with a strong Nonconformist tradition and a minority Welsh language. Scotland had its own parliament until the Act of Union of 1707 and retains its own church, its own distinctive legal system, and its own educational structure. Any visitor is immediately struck by the strong sense of Scottish identity. Ireland was partitioned by the Anglo-Irish Agreement of 1922, and the larger southern part peeled off to become first the Irish Free State and then the Republic of Ireland in 1949. The main *raison d'être* of the Protestant majority (many of whom are of Scottish descent) of deeply divided Northern Ireland is to maintain the 1800 Act of Union with mainland Britain; yet the flags, processions and religious dogmatics of these Irish Presbyterians are alien to Anglicans in England. Last, but not least, the big post-war wave of

17

Asian and West Indian immigration has brought with it a rich variety of different ethnic and cultural traditions to our national life.

This is not to deny the existence or the force of a 'British' national consciousness which transcends a specifically 'English' or indeed 'Scottish' or 'Welsh' identity. It has been developed by the economic, communications, media, educational and political revolutions of the last two hundred years and strengthened by two world wars. Undeniably, it draws on powerful unifying forces, especially the English language and parliamentary democracy. But if it is to retain its validity, then it has to discard those elements of the past which are no longer relevant.

The doctrine of parliamentary sovereignty, so confidently advocated by Dicey at the end of the nineteenth century and so fervently if defensively echoed by the anti-Europeans in the 1990s, is out of date. In terms of individual rights, it has proved inadequate to defend British citizens against the abuse of power by the executive. There have been twenty-one judgments (including seventeen since 1979) against the United Kingdom government in the European Court of Human Rights, the largest for any signatory nation. It has rightly been said that the list of British cases is 'long, controversial and far reaching'.[8] As the new democrats of Eastern Europe cannot fail to note, those Western European countries with written constitutions and a codified Bill of Rights have performed better than the United Kingdom which has relied exclusively on parliamentary sovereignty.

Buttressed by parliamentary sovereignty, the United Kingdom is arguably the most centralised state in the European Community. Things are organised differently in most other EC countries, where the rights and responsibilities of regional and local government are guaranteed by their constitutions. In this country, parliamentary sovereignty allows local government powers to be reduced or abolished (like the Greater London Council) and acts as a barrier to Scotland, Wales and, I would argue, the English regions being given the responsibilities which they ought to have.

The doctrine of parliamentary sovereignty is also at odds with British membership of the European Community. The Community which we joined in 1973 already had a considerable body of law which, by our decision to join, assumed precedence over our national law. So, when in 1989 the UK parliament was obliged to obey an interim order of the European Court to amend its legislative attempt to limit fishing by Spanish fishermen in British waters and thus evade the common fisheries policy, this necessity flowed from our membership of the EC. The 1987 Single European Act, signed by Mrs Thatcher, introduced qualified majority voting for the establishment and surveillance of the single-market programme which further reduced parliamentary sovereignty. The acceptance of the treaty on economic and monetary union and especially of a single European currency will continue to erode the sovereignty of the British parliament.

Only those who are wedded to this anachronistic concept see these developments purely in terms of loss. A more balanced analysis shows that, when we give up our own sovereignty, we also gain a share in a wider European sovereignty. Through our membership of common EC institutions and adherence to their policies, the British are able to influence Spanish fishermen, French car makers and even German monetary authorities. In short, the doctrine of parliamentary sovereignty, so proud a relic of our past, now represents an obstacle to making the best of the opportunities of the present and the future.


## First World Power

In November 1964, Labour's newly elected Prime Minister, Harold Wilson, proudly proclaimed to the City of London: 'We are a world power, and a world influence, or we are nothing'.[9] Until Britain joined the European Community in 1973, and arguably even until the resignation of Mrs Thatcher in November 1990, British politicians continually overstated Britain's position in the world. At the back of their minds, they could not forget that Britain had been the first world power.

It was Sir Walter Raleigh who presciently said: 'Who commands the sea commands trade; who commands the trade of the world commands its riches, and so commands the world itself.'[10] As a small group of islands off the north-west coast of Europe, Britain was well placed to become a world power. Its insularity protected it from the danger of overland attack, while its geographical position also enabled it to take advantage of the sixteenth-century shift in trade from the Mediterranean to the Atlantic. Its powerful fleet was both a guarantee against invasion and an instrument for the domination of the shipping lanes. After the 1688 settlement, the economic arm and the fighting arm of the country became 'mutually supporting organs of a grand strategy, predicated upon commercial expansion, colonial exploitation, domestic stability and insular security'.[11]

In the eighteenth century, Britain extended her colonial empire as a result of a series of wars with France. Napoleon's defeat in 1815 dislodged France from her position as the greatest of European powers. As the Prussian General August von Gneisenau remarked: 'Great Britain has no greater obligation than to this ruffian [Napoleon]. For through the events which he has brought about, England's greatness, prosperity and wealth have risen high. She is mistress of the sea and neither in this dominion nor in world trade has she now a single rival to fear.'[12]

The nineteenth century was the British century. The coming of the Industrial Revolution transformed the victor of the mercantilist struggles of the eighteenth century into a super power. At the time of the Great Exhibition at the Crystal Palace in 1850, Britain was the supreme industrial nation and the trading centre of the world. It produced two-thirds of the world's coal, about half its iron, five-sevenths of its steel, two-thirds of its hardware and about half its commercial cotton cloth. About 40 per cent of the entire world output of traded manufactured goods was produced within the country. It also became a vast exporter of capital to other countries. In what the Victorian historian, J. R. Seeley, called 'a fit of absence of mind', Britain also became the greatest empire the world has ever seen, expanding its territory between 1815 and 1865 at an average rate of 100,000 square miles a year.[13] After the imperialist explosion of the last quarter of the nineteenth century, a quarter of the globe was British. Commenting in his magisterial *Rise and Fall of the Great Powers*, Professor Paul Kennedy wrote: 'Like all other civilisations at the top of the wheel of fortune . . . the British could believe that their position was both "natural" and destined to continue. And just like all those other civilisations, they were in for a rude shock.'[14]

By 1914, Britain had been overtaken industrially by the United States and Germany and was being subjected to intense competition in its commercial, colonial and maritime spheres of influence. It was a world power on the defensive, with a built-in interest in preserving the *status quo*. Victory in two world wars (1914–18 and 1939–45) masked rather than reversed Britain's strategic and economic decline. In February 1945, the British Empire might appear at the Yalta Conference to be in the same league with the United States and the Soviet Union as one of the 'Big Three'. But the reality was that it was fatally overstretched. One of the first documents the incoming Labour government in August 1945 had to read was Keynes' memorandum, warning of a 'financial Dunkirk': its colossal trade gap, its weakened industrial base, the number and cost of its overseas establishments meant that Britain could no longer afford to be a world power.[15]

Seen in perspective, Britain's post-war dilemma has been how to manage its decline from world-power status and responsibility. Its strategic retreat has been compounded by economic weakness, so much so that British output has been overtaken not only by the two defeated powers, Japan and Germany, but also by France and, arguably, by Italy as well. Withdrawal from empire was carried out with some skill. The independence process, begun in 1947 on the Indian subcontinent by the Attlee government, was continued in Africa and elsewhere by Conservative administrations. In 1967, following devaluation, the Wilson government was forced to announce the end of the 'East of Suez' role and, by the early 1970s, most of the old global commitments had been abandoned. The Common-wealth still remained as a link with Britain's imperial past and a useful international forum, but it could not halt Britain's decline.

However, British post-war politicians of both major parties were slow to acknowledge that, if Britain still had some world interests, it was no longer a world power. Conservative leaders from Winston Churchill to Margaret Thatcher have remained irresistibly attracted to playing a role on the world stage rather than in Europe. The misleading message of Conservative elec-tion posters in 1987 was that 'Britain is great again', while Mrs Thatcher deliberately appealed to unrealistic aspirations with her claim that Britain was 'no ordinary country'.

The Labour Party, too, has had its illusions, also rooted in an overestimation of British influence. Hugh Gaitskell and Harold Wilson exaggerated the potential of the Commonwealth, while, on the left of the Party, there was a tendency to believe that Britain could act as a moral force throughout the world. This was no less a fantasy than the right-wing belief that Britain was still a world power. Such inflated assumptions about Britain's role played their part in shaping Labour's opposition to European integration.

### Standing Alone

A powerfully evocative theme in our history is that of Britain 'standing alone'. When Margaret Thatcher told the Germans that 'we are not easily dominated', she clearly had in mind the image of a brave and freedom-loving people, holding out alone in their island fortress against continental tyrants.

23

The great drama of 1940 seemed to confirm the history lessons. Churchill's magnificent speeches are still, over fifty years later, thrilling to hear: 'We shall fight on the beaches, we shall fight on the landing grounds, we shall fight in the fields and in the streets, we shall fight in the hills; we shall never surrender' (4 June 1940). 'Let us therefore brace ourselves to our duties and so bear ourselves that if the British Empire and its Commonwealth lasts for a thousand years men will say "This was their finest hour"' (18 June 1940). 'Never in the field of human conflict was so much owed by so many to so few' (5 September 1940).

Harold Macmillan, one of Churchill's lieutenants, movingly described the spirit of 1940:

> Even the humblest could feel that they were taking part in the making of history. As the new Armada was being prepared against us, we seemed indeed the heirs of Queen Elizabeth and her captains. All the great figures of the past – Drake, Raleigh, Marlborough, Chatham, Wolfe, Pitt, Nelson, Wellington – seemed alive again and almost standing at our side. The unity of the nation was complete and unshakeable.[16]

In an insouciant broadcast, J. B. Priestley told the Americans: 'We are at bay in our tight little island'. Typically going over the top, Arthur Mee exulted 'Now once again the Island stirs the world, and, whatever disasters may befall, the spirit of the Flag will save mankind.'[17]

Dorothy Sayers' wartime patriotic poem 'The English War' provides a valuable insight into the 'standing alone' frame of mind. It is uncompromisingly defiant, proudly 'offshore' and deeply suspicious of continental Europeans:[18]

> This is the war that England knows,
> When all the world holds but one man –
> King Philip of the galleons,
> Louis, whose light outshone the sun's,
> The conquering Corsican.
>
> When Europe, like a prison door,
> Clangs; and the swift, enfranchised sea
> Runs narrower than a village brook;
> And men who love us not, yet look
> To us for liberty;
>
> When no allies are left, no hope
> To count upon from alien hands,
> No waverers remain to woo,
> No more advice to listen to,
> And only England stands . . .

Enoch Powell put it more prosaically: 'Lucky for Europe that Britain was alone in 1940.'

Yet, not withstanding all the heroic symbolism of 1940, strategic and economic realities were somewhat different. If 'standing alone' depended on being an island (or rather a group of islands), many of the advantages of insularity had already been eroded by the coming of air power. In 1906, on hearing of one of the first successful flights, Lord Northcliffe told *The Daily Mail*: 'England is no longer an island. . . . It means the aerial chariots of a foe descending on British soil if war comes.'[19] By 1940 the sea which separated the British isles from the mainland of Europe was no longer so wide. It was the Royal Air Force not the Royal Navy which won the Battle of Britain.

'Standing alone' was also a purely defensive strategy. It may have prevented Hitler knocking Britain out of the war, as he had knocked out France. It did not – and could not – mean defeat for Germany. An accurate verdict on the strategic position at the end of 1940 is as follows: 'If the Battle of Britain had rendered impossible a German cross-Channel invasion, the imbalance of land forces made a British military entry into Europe quite out of the question.'[20] As Churchill fully understood, without American and Soviet participation victory over the Germans could not have been achieved. It was not only American and Russian troops that were needed to defeat Hitler. Equally vital was the supply of American food, raw materials, equipment, weapons and money. The much-vaunted British war effort was 'dependent on American strength as a patient on a life support machine'.[21] In economic terms, it was not so much a question of Britain 'standing alone' as being propped up.

In the 1990s, the idea of Britain 'standing alone' is out of the question. After victory in the Falklands in 1982, Mrs Thatcher attempted, mainly for domestic political purposes, to draw some kind of analogy between what she called the 'Falklands Factor' and 1940. 'We ... fought alone,' she said. She went on: 'Britain found herself again in the South Atlantic and will not look back from the victory she has won.' But the Falklands War was no more than a small colonial war, provoked by British negligence, fought against weak and incompetent opponents and won by an expedition force bolstered by American diplomatic, logistic and intelligence support. Despite the bravery of

British troops, the Falklands War could not, by any stretch of patriotic imagination, justify a revival of the policy of standing alone.

Today, Britain is a medium-sized European power and a member of the European Community. Politically and economically, it can no longer afford to be 'in a minority of one' (as it was all too often under Mrs Thatcher and also under John Major at Maastricht), certainly not to stand alone. In the 1990s, standing alone usually means being left behind.

**The Special Relationship**
One of the most enduring legacies of the Second World War has been Britain's 'special relationship' with the United States. The fall of France in 1940 was the traumatic event which pushed the British and Americans into a close alliance.[22] As France fell, Churchill appealed openly to Roosevelt for a US declaration of war. Although the Americans did not come into the war until after the Japanese attack on Pearl Harbor in December 1941, the French collapse was the key event which turned Britain from Europe and into the arms of the United States. After the war, the alliance of the two 'English speaking peoples' (as Churchill called them) was successfully transformed into a new arrangement between a senior and junior partner. The creation of NATO and the development of the Marshall Plan were very much a joint enterprise, with Bevin playing a major role alongside Marshall and Acheson in establishing the post-war structure of relationships between Western Europe and North America.

But the special relationship was always more important for Britain than for the United States, being in part a device used by a declining power to harness a rising power to serve its own ends. Harold Macmillan (like Winston Churchill half American by birth) spoke grandiloquently of Britain's playing Greece to America's Rome. In 1945 an anonymous poet gave a more down to earth, though equally patronising, view of the relationship: 'In Washington Lord Halifax / Once whispered to Lord Keynes / It's true they have the money bags / But we have all the brains.' The Nassau deal between Kennedy and Macmillan in December 1962 whereby the Americans agreed to provide the British with the Polaris missile system was indicative of British client status. The British remained in the nuclear game but only at the price of using an American delivery system.

In the 1970s and 1980s as British power declined and the American focus of interest shifted, the emphasis on a 'special relationship' seemed increasingly out of date. The United States is as much concerned with what happens in the Pacific, in Central and Latin America and in the Middle East as with events in Europe. And, in Europe, the United States looks not only to Britain but to the EC countries as a whole and especially to the more powerful united Germany. A Britain which still assumes that it enjoys a privileged position as a transatlantic intermediary between the United States and Europe risks falling between two stools, 'an increasingly irrelevant, if well loved, poor relation in Washington, and a "bad European" in a continent increasingly dominated by the Franco-German axis'.[23]

Ironically, American policy makers have been enthusiastic supporters of close British involvement with Western European integration, usually more

28

enthusiastic than the British themselves. In 1950, American Secretary of State, Dean Acheson, was in favour of British participation in the Schuman Plan. In 1956, President Eisenhower told Anthony Eden that he should take a less negative attitude to the Common Market negotiations. In 1961, President Kennedy strongly backed Macmillan's application to join the Common Market. He took the view that British membership would both strengthen the European Community (EC) and ensure that it would remain outward looking. Since British entry in 1973, the Americans have consistently urged that the British take a positive attitude within the EC. Even now, after the collapse of communism, they believe that a British presence is a guarantee that the EC will remain friendly to the United States.

In the 1940s and 1950s, the British were reluctant to commit themselves to building Europe, in part because they feared that it would encourage American isolationism. Once Britain became a member, their leaders clung to the special relationship, believing it gave them both a role within the Common Market as the country with the closest links with the USA, and kudos in Washington as the most pro-American of EC members. In 1978 James Callaghan attempted to play honest broker between Chancellor Schmidt and President Carter in the run-up to the Bonn summit. In 1984 at Camp David Mrs Thatcher used her influence with President Reagan on behalf of the Europeans to set conditions on Reagan's 'Star Wars' project. In 1990–91 the Gulf War, in which the British made the biggest European contribution in military terms, once again underlined old ties. Mrs Thatcher's admonition to President Bush to stand firm – 'Don't go wobbly, George' – was not only a vintage 'Thatcherism'; it also represented a good example of how British political leaders see the 'special relationship' as entitling them to hand out advice to the Americans.

But, in reality, the 'special relationship' is an anachronism. The British will always have a close relationship with the Americans. We share a common language. The United States remains a big market for British goods. There is a considerable American investment in the United Kingdom. But the idea that we can continue to count on a *special* relationship or that it should be at the expense of closer involvement in the EC is misconceived, a product of our past which is irrelevant to our future.

### No European Entanglements

When Anthony Crosland addressed the European Parliament as foreign secretary in January 1977, he said that British membership of the European Community represented Britain's first permanent peacetime engagement on the continent of Europe since the Reformation.[24] Even allowing for an element of politician's hyperbole, Crosland was pointing to an enduring axiom of British foreign policy. It was to preserve the European balance of power as far as possible, but to avoid any long-term entanglement on the mainland of Europe. As Lord Palmerston put it, Britain had permanent interests but no permanent allies.

To generations of British political leaders, the Continent meant trouble. In the sixteenth century, there was the attempt by the Spanish to dominate Europe. Over the next two centuries, the French made their bid for hegemony. Then after 1870 it was the turn of the

Germans. To justify his anti-Hitler policy, Churchill wrote in 1936:

> British policy for four hundred years has been to oppose the strongest power in Europe by weaving together a combination of other countries strong enough to face the bully. Sometimes, it is Spain, sometimes the French monarchy, sometimes the French Empire, sometimes Germany. I have no doubt who it is now. . . . It is thus through the centuries we have kept our liberties and maintained our life and power.[25]

In 1914 and again in 1939, the British went to war to prevent what they saw as a German attempt to establish a European hegemony. After the wars were over and the Germans defeated, British politicians remained ambivalent about becoming too closely involved in the affairs of the Continent. Keynes said: 'Europe is apart and England is not of her flesh and body.'[26] Provided the Continental balance was maintained, the British tried to remain offshore islanders.

Even Churchill's fine speech at Zurich in September 1946, in which he called for the reconciliation of France and Germany and the creation of a United States of Europe, was in the classic tradition of British foreign policy. He wanted to unite Western Europe as a counterbalance to the post-war ambitions of the Soviet Union. But in Churchill's view, Western European unity did not imply too close a British involvement with that union. If it was a choice between the Continent of Europe and the 'open sea', Britain should opt for the 'open sea'.

It was this sceptical caste of mind which the post-war

generation of British leaders brought to the problems of Europe. At a time when a decline in power and a shift in interests argued strongly for greater British involvement in the mainland of Europe, British statesmen hung back. They were misled by history.

# – 2 –

# 'Offshore' Attitudes

'Storm in channel: Continent Isolated'. The isolationist sentiments behind the words, which, according to reliable sources, appeared on London evening newspaper billboards sometime in the 1930s, are still prevalent today. Despite nearly twenty years of European Community membership, too many of the British are insular, psychologically as well as geographically detached from the continent. They remain 'offshore' islanders.

In one sense, it is illegitimate to make generalisations about nations or about how they view other people. Theodore Zeldin, in his brilliant study of the French, puts the dilemma succinctly 'To describe a nation of 54 million, still less one of 220 million, in a single phrase . . . is a natural reaction in the face of the complexity of the world, but it is a habit born of despair, which persists because there seems no obvious way of avoiding it.'[1] Clearly, there are numerous exceptions to my generalisation about British insularity. The Scots, the Welsh and the Irish are, in many respects, different from the English. There is also another tradition which stresses the links with the Continent and which I discuss in the second part of the book. And there is strong evidence of a gradual shift in overall British attitudes towards the EC also examined in that second half of the book. But although opinion *is* changing, a substantial proportion of the public is still uneasy with foreigners and sceptical about the EC.

## From Patriotism to Xenophobia

In 1940 at the height of the blitz, with German bombs raining down on London, George Orwell wrote his celebrated polemic, *The Lion and the Unicorn*, which contained one of the most perceptive descriptions of the national character ever made. Both a radical socialist and an instinctive patriot, Orwell fully understood the force of national feeling: 'One cannot see the modern world as it is unless one recognizes the overwhelming strength of patriotism ... as a positive force there is nothing to set beside it.'[2] He described England as a family with the wrong members in control, 'A rather stuffy Victorian family, with not many black sheep in it but with all its cupboards bursting with skeletons ... still it is a family. It has its private language and its common memories, and at the approach of an enemy it closes its ranks.'[3] One passage in Orwell's essay is especially apposite today:

> In England patriotism takes different forms in different classes, but it runs like a connecting thread through nearly all of them. ... As a positive emotion it is stronger in the middle class than in the upper class. ... In the working class patriotism is profound, but it is unconscious. The working man's heart does not leap when he sees a Union Jack. But the famous 'insularity' and 'xenophobia' of the English is far stronger in the working class

than in the bourgeoisie. . . . Even when they are
obliged to live abroad for years they refuse either
to accustom themselves to foreign food or to learn
foreign languages. . . . The insularity of the English, their refusal to take foreigners seriously, is a
folly that has to be paid for very heavily from time
to time. . . . At bottom it is the same quality of the
English character that repels the tourist and keeps
out the invader.[4]

Orwell puts his finger on the problem. The strong
patriotism of the English, that national loyalty which
has been shaped by their exceptional history and which
in time of crisis or war has helped the country to
survive, can spill over into irrational jingoism and
contempt for foreigners. In the wrong hands and in the
wrong circumstances, the spirit of Dunkirk can degen-
erate into the anti-German hysteria of 1915 or the
horror of Heysel stadium, where violence by Liverpool
football supporters was responsible for the deaths of
thirty-nine Italian fans.

English nationalism, as it developed in Tudor times,
was frequently xenophobic. In 1554, there was spon-
taneous opposition to Queen Mary's 'Spanish' marriage
to Philip II. Later, in Elizabeth's reign, Protestant
propagandists like John Foxe whipped up popular
feelings against foreigners by gruesome descriptions of
the methods of the Spanish and French Inquisitions.
The papal bull of 1570 excommunicating Queen Elizabeth, the St Bartholomew's Night massacre of French
Huguenots in Paris of 1572, the 1584 assassination of
William the Silent, the attempted Catholic plots against
Elizabeth, and, above all, the Spanish Armada, served
to inflame jingoistic sentiment.

Elizabeth's Lord Chancellor, Sir Christopher Hatton, in his opening speech to the 1589 parliament, made rabble-rousing attacks on the pope, 'that wolfish bloodsucker'; on the king of Spain, 'that insatiable tyrant'; and on English Catholic priests, 'bloody priests and false traitors' who acted on behalf of foreigners against their native country.[5] By 1603, Lord Burghley was urging his son, Robert Cecil: 'And suffer not their sons to pass the Alps, for they shall learn nothing but pride, blasphemy and atheism'.[6]

Even that great universalist Shakespeare at times reflects the fervent nationalism of his age. His historical plays are spattered with tributes to England and the English. England is a 'sea walled garden', 'this fortress built by nature for herself'; a 'waterwalled bulwark'; 'Neptune's park'. The English are an exceptional and courageous people: 'Submission Dauphin! Tis a mere French word. We English warriors wot not what it means'; 'Come the three corners of the world in arms, and we shall shock them'; 'This happy breed of men'. *Henry V* is not a critique of feudal aggression but a great patriotic tale of how the brave few, the English led by a hero king, triumphed over the arrogant many, the French: 'O noble English, that could entertain with half their forces the full pride of France'; 'We few, we happy few, we band of brothers'; 'More than abounding valour in our English'. The French are portrayed as effete, over confident, vainglorious: 'Yet, forgive me, God, that I do brag thus! This your air of France hath blown that vice in me'; 'Proud of their numbers, secure in soul, the confident and over-lusty French'; 'For our approach shall so much dark the field that England shall crouch down in fear, and yield'.

To the xenophobic strain in English nationalism,

36

imperialism added the element of racial superiority. The fact that at the end of the nineteenth century a little over 6000 British officials were able to govern almost 300 million Indians, with the help of not much more than 70,000 British soldiers, seemed to be conclusive proof of superiority.[7] Rudyard Kipling, the brilliant bard of empire, might praise the civilising mission of imperialism:

> Take up the White Man's burden –
> Send forth the best ye breed –
> God bind your sons to exile
> To serve your captive's need

But, though Kipling supported the spread of law, literacy and communications, he took for granted the superiority of the British not only over those they ruled but also over other European peoples. If it was the White Man's burden to teach subject peoples, neither the Germans, the Russians nor even the French were up to it. Only the British, and possibly the Americans (Kipling had an American wife), could do the job. It was Cecil Rhodes, much admired by Kipling who said 'Always remember that you are an Englishman, and consequently have won first prize in the lottery of life.'

Another strand in British attitudes is their notorious insularity. Their geographical position on the periphery of Europe combined with their unique historical experience has meant that, until comparatively recently, the British have remained largely ignorant of those who lived beyond our shore. Indeed, before the stationing of American troops in Britain during the Second World

War, the only mass experience of foreigners was acquired when the British left their islands to fight either on the mainland of Europe or further afield to extend or defend their far-flung empire.[8]

As early as 1500, a Venetian wrote:

> They think that there are no other men than themselves, and no other world but England. And whenever they see a handsome foreigner, they say that he looks like an Englishman and that it is a great pity that he should not be an Englishman, and when they partake of any delicacy with a foreigner, they ask him whether such a thing is made in his country.[9]

Even members of the ruling élite, with opportunities to travel, were often profoundly insular. The biographer of Sir Edward Grey, the British foreign secretary at the time of the First World War, describes him as a 'classically insular Foreign Secretary whose distinguished tenure of office had been untouched by personal first hand knowledge of the European countries with which he had so frequently to deal.'[10] In 1951, when Selwyn Lloyd was appointed minister of state at the Foreign Office, he admitted to the prime minister, Winston Churchill, that he did not speak any foreign language, had never visited a foreign country except during the war, and did not like foreigners.[11] As the aristocratic Uncle Matthew in Nancy Mitford's *The Pursuit of Love* so crudely put it, 'abroad is unutterably bloody and foreigners are fiends'.

Since the Second World War, the British have had far more contacts with other cultures than before. Two developments have transformed the situation. The first is the large-scale influx of immigrants from the Indian subcontinent and the West Indies. The second great change is the spectacular expansion of tourism, particularly to the Continent of Europe. The vast majority of the British have visited at least one country on the Continent, while over 50 per cent have visited three or more.[12] Over half the population now wears continental clothes, consumes Continental fruit, vegetables, wine and cheese, and, at some time or other, has had a Continental meal. Travel and trade (see Chapter 7) has clearly helped break down barriers. More than a third of Britons have friends, acquaintances or business contacts in other European countries. More people now feel closer to the Continentals than they do to the Australians or the Americans.

But there still exists an element of distrust of the Continental Europeans, which travel has apparently not yet eradicated. Although France and Spain are among the countries most frequently visited by the British, the French and the Spanish are the nations whom they most distrust.[13] The French and the Spanish feel the same about the British. Part of the explanation for this mutual feeling may lie in the nature of mass travel and package holidays which means that the British move around in their own exclusive groups. What makes matters worse is that, because of their ignorance of foreign languages, most Britons are unable to communicate with the Continentals. In addition, there is undoubtedly still a xenophobic strain in some of the British abroad which, as with the lager louts in Spain or the hooligans at European football matches, has led to aggression and violence.

The tabloid press does not hesitate to exploit British xenophobia for its own purpose. The *Sun* is in a class of its own for abusive chauvinism.[14] The paper that during the Falklands War brought the nation the headlines 'Stick it up your Junta' and 'Gotcha' when the *Belgrano* was sunk is equally tasteless when it comes to the Continental Europeans. During the 1984 'Lamb war', the *Sun* told puerile anti-French jokes: 'Why are there so many tree lined streets in France? So the German army can march in the shade'; and 'What do you call a pretty girl in France? A tourist'. When the *Sun*'s German equivalent, *Bild* criticised British holiday louts in Majorca in 1987, the *Sun* counter-attacked with the splash, 'The *Sun* invades Germany', next to a picture of Churchill giving the V sign. Under the sub-head 'Wapping task force to teach the Krauts holiday manners', the *Sun* screamed, 'It's war folks! Your patriotic *Sun* was last night assembling a Wapping task force to invade Germany – and give those lout Krauts a lesson to remember'. When England played Germany in the 1990 World Cup, the *Sun*'s headline again recalled the war: 'Herr we go. Herr we go. We beat them in 1945. Now for 1990.' At the height of the row over Mrs Thatcher's European policy which led to her downfall in November 1990, the *Sun* launched a campaign against the President of the European Commission under the headline 'Up Yours Delors'. It urged its readers to tell 'the feelthy French to frog off'. It went on:

They insult us, burn our lambs, flood our country with dodgy food and plot to abolish the dear old pound. Now it is your turn to kick them in the Gauls. We want you to tell Froggie Common Market Chief Jacques Delors exactly what you think of him and his countrymen. At the stroke of noon tomorrow, we invite all true blue Brits to face France and yell 'Up Yours, Delors'.

The tardiness of most of Britain's European partners in making a contribution to the UN operation in the Gulf gave the tabloid press a field day. A *Daily Express* editorial ('The Price of Courage') on 23 January 1991 had three lines of attack. First Britain alone had taken its responsibilities seriously. Second, the rich Europeans (particularly Germany) should have been prepared to make a greater financial contribution. Third, the idea of European political union had been fatally weakened: 'We have not shirked our responsibilities. Nor must our partners. Especially those who are keenest on telling us what a central role the EC is about to play in the world.' Even the *Mirror*, normally staunchly pro-European, joined in the criticism. The *Sun*, which announced, 'We are so proud to be British' weighed in with vitriolic outbursts against both Germany and France. Under the headline 'Menace of the Germans', it put in the boot: 'At every turn, Germany has gone her own way. It has been *Deutschland uber alles* – and everyone else can take a jump in the Rhine.' When it interviewed the German Ambassador ('The Hun meets the *Sun*'), it asked him, 'Why are the Germans behaving in such a cowardly manner during the Gulf crisis?' The French, who, like the British, had sent troops to the Gulf, were taken to task for President Mitterrand's last-minute peace initiative: 'There is only one thing worse than having the messieurs as your enemy. That is to have them as your friend.' *Sun* journalists argue that the paper's jingoism should not be taken too seriously. But any paper which consistently sells over three and a half million copies daily must have some impact. At the least, it makes aggressive chauvinism respectable and legitimises the crudest kind of national stereotyping.

### 'Those Bloody Frogs Have Let Us Down'

John Stuart Mill once wrote to de Tocqueville: 'It is only natural that the English should not be able to understand France, just as the French are unable to understand England.' The British are deeply ambivalent about the French. On the one hand, they tend to distrust them and consider them arrogant. On the other hand, they also find them stylish, sexy and intriguingly immoral.[15] Typically, they call a condom a 'French letter' (the French call it *une capote anglaise*) and talk about liaisons and affairs. Laurence Sterne's *A Sentimental Journey*, written in 1768, tantalisingly but revealingly concluded: 'So that when I stretched out my hand, I caught hold of the *fille de chambre's*'.

A simple explanation of the British distrust of the French is that for centuries the two countries have been enemies. From the Hundred Years War of the fourteenth and fifteenth centuries to the wars of the eighteenth century, culminating in the struggle against Napoleon (often called the 'Second Hundred Years War'), France was Britain's main rival. To a considerable extent, English nationalism and English culture defined itself as Francophobe.

When sixteenth- and seventeenth-century antiquarians 'discovered' the freedom-loving Anglo-Saxons as ancestors, they discarded the Normans as Continental, Frenchified conquerors. In contrast to the tyrant William the Conqueror, Anglo-Saxon King Alfred was the good king who had respected his subjects' liberties. The anti-French bias of this new Anglo-Saxon myth was made clear by John Aylmer, Marian exile and later Elizabeth's Bishop of London. Writing from Switzerland in 1550 he berated 'the effeminate Frenchmen: stoute in bragge but nothing in deed', dismissing their contribution to English culture contemptuously: 'We have a few hunting terms and pedlars French in the louyse lawe, brought in by the Normans, yet remainying: But the language and customs bee English and Saxonyshe.'[16]

Eighteenth-century English culture had a strong Gallophobe streak.[17] Novelists like Smollet and Fielding, dramatists like Garrick and Foote, artists like Hogarth and Gillray, even the great Dr Johnson rejected the cosmopolitan values of the French as insincere, artificial and corrupt. In *The Countess's Morning Levee*, the fourth picture in his *Marriage à la Mode* series, William Hogarth condemned the worship of un-English fashions by caricaturing ridiculous-looking foreign musicians, a French hairdresser, a French novel and a voluptuous Correggio on the wall. In one of his plays, Samuel Foote urges the rejection of French culture:

For other views attract our modern race
Tulles, toupees, trinkets, bags, brocades and lace;
a flaunting form, and a fictitious face.
Rouse! Re-assume! refuse a Gallic reign
Nor let their arts win that their arms could never gain.

The message is clear. Honest, plain John Bull, (an eighteenth-century creation) should discard dangerous French fashions.

The French revolution accentuated English fears. There were those like the Whig politician, Charles James Fox, the revolutionary propagandist, Thomas Paine, and the poets, William Wordsworth and Percy Bysshe

Shelley, who looked on it as a new dawn. But Edmund Burke, in his celebrated *Reflections on the Revolution in France*, published in 1790, spoke for most of the political class when he warned of the dangers of revolution and championed the 'inherited' rights and institutions of England:

> France, when she let loose the reins of regal authority, doubled the licence, of a ferocious dissoluteness in manners, and of an insolent irreligion in opinions and practices; and has extended through all ranks of life, as if she were communicating some privilege, or laying open some secluded benefit, all the unhappy corruptions that usually were the disease of wealth and power.[18]

Division of interest and cultural rejection were now reinforced by ideological conflict.

But, after the end of the Napoleonic Wars, Britain and France never fought again and, in the twentieth century, enmity has been replaced by alliance. The Anglo-French agreement of April 1904, the so-called *entente cordiale*, though not an official alliance, settled outstanding colonial differences. Then in the 1914–18 war, the British and the French fought side by side against the Germans. In 1939, they went to war together against Hitler. Since the Second World War, the two nations have remained allies. Today, France is a fellow EC member and major trading partner. Yet some of the old resentments still linger.

The experience of fighting on the same side in the 1914–18 war did not always bring the two peoples closer together. According to Orwell, the reaction of the British troops was that 'they brought back a hatred of all Europeans, except the Germans whose courage they admired. In four years on French soil they did not even acquire a liking for wine.'[19] In A. G. Macdonell's gentle satire *England their England* published in 1933, an old man in a country pub explained: 'We fought on the wrong side. . . . Those Frenchies were never any use to us. My father saw the beacons on the downs of Sussex when Boney was on the other side. The Germans never did us any harm. It's they Frenchies.'[20]

The sudden collapse of France in 1940 and the unilateral capitulation to the Germans not only dumbfounded the British but also aroused old suspicions. David Wright's poem on the fall of France summed up British feelings: 'Day in London, 18 June / There by a stone museum lion I'd / seen a man close a newspaper: / "Those bloody frogs have let us down"'.[21] In 1942 Mrs Thatcher's father, Alderman Roberts, told Grantham Council that France was 'corrupt from top to bottom'.[22] King George VI was relieved to be rid of the French. He wrote to his mother that he felt happier that there were no allies to be polite to or pamper.

After the war, Anglo-French relations were ruffled by the British decisions not to join either the European Coal and Steel Community (created in 1951) or the Common Market (set up in 1958); by the disastrous Anglo-French Suez expedition of 1956; and above all by the return to power in 1958 of General Charles de Gaulle. Twice in the 1960s, following the decision in 1961 of the Macmillan government to apply for membership of the European Community, de Gaulle brutally extinguished British hopes of joining.

De Gaulle was, to a considerable extent, Churchill's creation. It was Churchill who, after the collapse of France, set de Gaulle up in London as leader of the Free

French (Churchill called him the 'Constable of France') and who, despite considerable irritation with de Gaulle's monumental pride, continued to support him in the face of American opposition. De Gaulle's personal attitude towards the British will be considered in the next chapter. But what needs to be said here is that he drew the conclusion from his wartime experience that Britain was a European power in name only: if asked to decide between the United States and Europe, the British would always choose the United States. In his war memoirs, he recalled a conversation he had had with Churchill in the dark days of 1940: 'Mr Churchill and I agreed modestly in drawing from the events which had smashed the west this commonplace but final conclusion: when all is said and done, Great Britain is an island; France, the cape of a continent; America, another world.'[23] These geographical assumptions shaped de Gaulle's post-war policies. His plan was to rid Europe of Anglo-Saxon predominance and to establish a bloc of European states, under French leadership, which could act as an arbiter between the Soviet and Anglo-American camps.[24]

Given de Gaulle's geo-political fixations, the only possible chance, perhaps not a very strong one, of getting him to change his mind about British entry was either to convince him that the British were now prepared to accept their European destiny, or to isolate him so completely that he would not feel able to block their entry. It was of no use trying to appeal to wartime comradeship, or thinking that de Gaulle would negotiate, as the Conservative prime minister Harold Macmillan did, or hoping, like the Labour prime minister, Harold Wilson, that a tour of European capitals in company with his foreign secretary, George Brown, would somehow bring the walls of Jericho tumbling down.

Macmillan also made two tactical mistakes which played into de Gaulle's hands. He allowed negotiations to drag on into the autumn of 1962, by which time de Gaulle's hand had been strenghtened by a successful parliamentary election in France, and he signed the December Nassau deal (by which President Kennedy agreed to give Britain US Polaris missiles), thus affording de Gaulle the pretext to say that once again Britain had chosen the United States before Europe. When in January 1963 at one of his dramatic press conferences he announced a French veto on British membership, the French President grandly explained that Britain had not yet accepted a 'European vocation'. 'England,' announced de Gaulle, was 'insular, maritime, bound by her trade, her market, her supplies, to countries that are very diverse and often very far away. . . . How can England, as she lives, as she produces, as she trades, be incorporated into the Common Market?'[25] He also referred to the Nassau Agreement as further evidence that we were not ready for membership. Macmillan's strategy lay in ruins.

De Gaulle's dismissal in November 1967 of Harold Wilson's attempt to join was even more crushing. Wilson had mistakenly boasted that he would be able to get on with de Gaulle better than Macmillan had: 'We won't take no for an answer'. The reality was different. De Gaulle poured contempt on the Wilson application. It was like the 'fifth act of a play during which Britain's very diverse attitudes to the Common Market came, one after another, without seeming to be alike'.

Anglo-French relations reached their post-war nadir at the time of the Soames affair in February 1969. A curious conversation between the British ambassador, Christopher Soames, and Charles de Gaulle took place at a private lunch during which the General seemed to be suggesting scrapping the Common Market and replacing it by a free trade area. An account of the conversation was leaked by Harold Wilson, hoping to earn credit with other EC members, to the then German chancellor, Kurt Kiesinger. A French official accused the British of 'diplomatic terrorism', while the British revealed that their version of the conversation had been 'authorised' by the French government.

With the departure of de Gaulle in 1969 and Britain's entry to the Common Market in 1973, the Anglo-French climate improved. Prime Minister Edward Heath established a cordial relationship with President Georges Pompidou, while Prime Minister James Callaghan got on reasonably well with President Valéry Giscard d'Estaing. But with the advent of Mrs Thatcher to power in 1979 relations again became strained.

Mrs Thatcher, an English version of de Gaulle, both distrusted Giscard and found him supercilious. In his turn, Giscard found her egotistical and xenophobic, 'une petite bourgeoise provinciale'. In his memoirs, he relates how he breakfasted with Mrs Thatcher at her hotel suite at the Venice Summit in 1980. Allowing Mrs Thatcher to talk, Giscard decided

> to penetrate her mental process and gain an understanding of her inhibitions. I realised her immense pride in running the United Kingdom and I realised that she looked on other countries with a deep condescension, apparent not in her courteous manner but in her occasionally brusque and categorical judgements . . . I divined the fundamental

trait in her character: for her, her interlocutor had
no dialectical existence.[26]

Although he was a socialist, Mrs Thatcher's relations
with Giscard's successor, François Mitterrand, were
relatively cordial on a personal level. But Mitterrand,
who once said that Mrs Thatcher combined the mouth
of Marilyn Monroe with the eyes of Caligula, became
so frustrated by her diplomatic style that he twice
proposed a 'two-speed' Europe, with Britain either in
the slow lane or being given a special status of her own.
Mrs Thatcher got her own back on President Mitterrand
during the lavish French Revolution bicentenary cele-
brations in Paris in July 1989. Patronisingly she told Le
Monde: 'Every nation can decide how it wants to
celebrate this kind of event. You had your Eiffel Tower
a century ago. Why should you not amuse yourself this
time in the manner you wish?' She then went on to
deliver a stinging ideological rebuke: 'The rights of man
did not originate in France. . . . We had our Magna
Carta in 1215, the Bill of Rights in the seventeenth
century and our quiet revolution of 1688, when parliament imposed its will on the monarchy. More discretely
than you, we celebrated this event last year.' In Burkean
tones, she pointed out that the French Revolution had
led to the terror and to Napoleon, who had tried to
unite Europe by force: 'The Revolution was a fantastic
event, but was also a period of terror. When one reads
the history books, one is horrified by many aspects of
this period. Some of the French are as horrified as we
are.'[27]

But it was with the French president of the EC
Commission, Jacques Delors, that Mrs Thatcher clashed
most frequently and openly. To her, Delors was in a

category of his own. He was not only a Frenchman and a socialist; he also had the temerity to challenge Mrs Thatcher on her home ground. In September 1988, he made a notable and highly persuasive speech to the TUC Conference in Bournemouth in favour of the idea of a more socially responsible Europe. Mrs Thatcher's Bruges speech later that month was a direct riposte to Delors: 'We have not worked all these years to free Britain from the paralysis of Socialism only to see it creep through the back door of central control and bureaucracy in Brussels.' She began to refer to the 'Carolingian Empire', while another English nationalist, Enoch Powell, even accused Delors of wanting to be crowned 'emperor'. Jacques Delors' support for the Social Charter and his subsequent advocacy of a single European currency confirmed Thatcherite suspicions not only of the European Commission but also of the French. Like the Germans and other continental Europeans, they were not to be trusted. Yet it cannot be sensible to conduct our relations with France on the basis of distrust and prejudice. In the new Europe, with a more powerful Germany and a reduced American presence, it will be very much in the British interest to develop a constructive relationship with such an important neighbour.

### The 'Uppity' Germans

During the first half of the twentieth century the British had good reason to fear the Germans. Since 1945, however, the emergence of a democratic and peaceful Germany has helped to change our attitudes. The achievement of German reunification in 1990 may have given rise to publicly expressed misgivings about

German intentions, particularly by some Conservative politicians. But the majority of the British remain convinced that a united Germany presents no threat.[28] They are also impressed by the way the Germans run their economy and by their overall efficiency.[29] Their main criticism, according to the polls, is that the latter are arrogant and somewhat dull.[30]

Until the rise of the Anglo-German antagonism at the end of the nineteenth century, dynastic, political, cultural and economic links between Britain and the northern states of Germany were close. From 1714 onwards the British monarchs were Hanoverians, who spoke German, married Germans and were closely involved in German politics. In the middle of the eighteenth century, Frederick the Great of Prussia, whose mother was a sister of George II of Britain, became our main Continental ally. During the Seven Years War (1756–63), while British generals won decisive victories over the French in Canada and India, Frederick's military genius, assisted by a large British subsidy and an Anglo-Hanoverian army in north-western Germany, kept the armies of France, Russia and Austria at bay in Europe. In the Napoleonic wars, Prussia was more often than not allied to Britain. At the battle of Waterloo it was the opportune arrival in late evening of the Prussian army, under Marshal Blücher, which, as Wellington acknowledged, sealed Napoleon's fate.

In the first half of the nineteenth century, a third of Britain's European exports went to the German states.[31] The trade balance was very much in our favour. Germans bought sugar, spice, coffee and tea from our colonies, and, as Germany industrialised, coal from our mines, steam engines, textile machines, rails and other manufactures from our factories. German merchants and financiers set up businesses in important industrial centres such as Manchester and Bradford.

The cultural balance was more to Germany's advantage. British historians admired the scholarship of Ranke and Mommsen. They also decided that the British were apparently of 'Teutonic' stock and that our language, laws and customs were of Germanic origin. Even parliament was apparently based on the German folk moot. 'The German element is the paternal element in our system, natural and political' wrote one prominent constitutional historian.[32] British poets, novelists and philosphers were profoundly impressed by the German intellectual flowering.[33] Samuel Coleridge, who visited Germany in 1797, led the way. He translated Schiller, was fascinated by Goethe and studied Kant. Thomas Carlyle, the chief Germanist of his age, wrote biographies of Schiller and Frederick the Great, translated Goethe and was strongly influenced throughout his life by German literature and philosophy. Later, in the middle of the nineteenth century, George Eliot and her husband, G. H. Lewes, introduced German thinking, including the ideas of Hegel, to the British academic world. George Eliot wrote that 'no one in this day . . . studies any subject without having recourse to German books'.

German unification, however, led to a cooling in Anglo-German relations. It was not that the British were against the principle of unification. But they were shocked by the methods used by Otto von Bismarck, the Prussian statesman, to achieve it. The successful Prussian wars against Denmark (1864), Austria (1866) and France (1870), which united Germany by force, alienated British political opinion. At a conference in 1864 on the Schleswig-Holstein question, the British foreign secretary, Lord Clarendon, is said to have left the room overcome with an almost physical nausea at Bismarck's lack of moral scruple. In 1875, Queen Victoria, whose daughter Vicky was married to the Prussian crown prince, wrote to her that 'Bismarck is so over-bearing, violent, grasping and unprincipled that no one can stand it, and all agreed that he was becoming like the first Napoleon whom Europe had to join in PUTTING DOWN.'[34] However, if Bismarck's unscrupulous diplomacy upset the British, he had no wish to fight Britain or indeed any other country once unification had been achieved.

It was the rapid growth of German economic and military power under his successors which so alarmed the British and led to the 1914–18 war. Whereas Britain produced over twice as much steel as Germany in 1860, by 1914 it produced less than half. British leaders perceived the new German might, particularly the expansion of their fleet, as a direct threat to their position as a world-wide imperial power. In a famous memorandum to his foreign secretary, the British diplomat, Eyre Crowe (who was married to a German), warned that 'Germany was hostile to Britain and distinctly aims at playing on the world's political stage a much larger and much more dominant part than she finds allotted to herself under the present distribution of material power'.[35] Jingoistic attacks in the British press reflected the official unease at the German intentions; it also fed popular xenophobia. According to Lord Northcliffe, proprietor of *The Daily Mail*, the average Briton liked a 'good hate'. He proceeded to provide one daily, often at the expense of the Germans.

Virulent anti-Germanism was at its height during and immediately after the First World War. Rudyard Kipling, whose son was killed in Flanders, wrote in *The Daily Express*:

> One thing we must get into our thick heads is that whenever the German man or woman gets a suitable culture to thrive in he or she means death and loss to civilized people, precisely as germs of any disease . . . mean death or loss to mankind.[36]

The armistice of November 1918 was greeted with cries of 'Hang the Kaiser!' and 'Squeeze Germany until the pips squeak!' But the hate at home was not always felt at the front. British soldiers often came back from the war with a grudging respect for the bravery and effectiveness of their German counterparts.

Progressive opinion in Britain soon swung against the harsh settlement imposed on Germany by the Treaty of Versailles.[37] J. M. Keynes wrote a devastating polemic against financial reparations in his famous book *The Economic Consequences of the Peace*, in which he argued that Europe would only prosper if Germany was returned to its former economic strength. It was guilt over the post-war treatment of Germany which was one of the underlying factors which shaped the policy of appeasement. Churchill called the Second World War 'the Unnecessary War', in the sense that it could have been avoided if Hitler had been confronted earlier. But leading Conservative politicans, particularly Prime Minister Neville Chamberlain, thought that they could negotiate with Hitler. Even the Labour Party, which opposed him from the beginning as a Fascist, failed to support the necessary rearmament. It may have been highly laudable to want reconciliation with Germany in the 1920s but it was disastrous to try and appease Hitler in the 1930s. Hitler was an evil warmonger who could only be stopped by force.

In the bitterness of war, British public opinion made little distinction between the Nazis and the Germans. Intellectual justification for this view was given by the historian Rohan Butler in his book *The Roots of National Socialism*, which tried to establish connections between Nazi philosophising and German philosophy.[38] My Oxford history tutor, A. J. P. Taylor, wrote in his *The Course of German History* that 'it was no more a mistake for the German people to end up with Hitler than it is an accident when a river flows into the sea'.[39] But others argued that, though unspeakable things had been done in their name, it was unjust to condemn a whole people. If Churchill once made the quip that 'the Germans are either at your throat or at your feet', in his war speeches he blamed Hitler and the Nazis rather than the Germans. As early as 1946, in his Zurich speech, he said that there could be no revival of Europe without 'a spiritually great Germany'.

After the war the British made an important contribution to the building of German democracy.[40] They helped to establish the German electoral system (a compromise between the proportional representation of the Weimar Republic and the British 'first past the post' arrangements); they backed German federalism; they insisted on a non-political civil service; and they advised that German trade unions should be set up on an industrial basis. German friends sometimes remark that it would have been better for the British if they had applied these ideas to their own institutions.

In the 1950s, despite left-wing opposition to German rearmament, British governments helped prepare the way for German participation in the Western Alliance.

Eden's initiative, which led to the setting up of the Western European Union, was decisive. In the 1960s, Britain's campaign to join the European Community was given consistent support by Germany. British entry in 1973 owed much to the strong backing of Federal Chancellor, Willy Brandt. By the end of the 1980s, Germany was not only Britain's NATO ally and fellow member of the EC but also our chief (though the balance was very much in Germany's favour) trading partner.

But despite these close political and economic ties, Anglo-German relations were not as close as they should have been. Mrs Thatcher's personal relations with Helmut Schmidt and Helmut Kohl are considered in the next chapter. What needs to be said here is that it was Mrs Thatcher's hostile attitude towards European integration that was the main reason for the coolness between London and Bonn. The Germans found her anti-European attitude profoundly irritating. The other problem was Mrs Thatcher's visceral anti-Germanism. Her formative years were during the war and she never thew off her distrust of the Germans. Reunification aroused all her old fears. The bizarre Ridley affair brought matters into the open.

In a notorious interview in *The Spectator* in July 1990, Nicholas Ridley, then secretary of state for industry and a leading supporter of Mrs Thatcher in the cabinet, warned about the dangers of Germany becoming 'so uppity'.[41] He described economic and monetary union as 'a German racket designed to take over the whole of Europe'. He went on: 'This rushed take-over by the Germans on the worst possible basis, with the French behaving like poodles to the Germans, is absolutely intolerable.' When asked whether Chancellor Kohl was not preferable to Adolf Hitler, Ridley replied: 'I am not sure I wouldn't rather have the shelters and the chance to fight back than simply being taken over by economics.' After some delay, Ridley, who was in Budapest on an official mission, was forced to resign.

However, the leaking in *The Independent on Sunday* of the minutes of a confidential Chequers meeting of mostly Second World War historians, at which Mrs Thatcher and the foreign secretary, Douglas Hurd, were present, revealed that his doubts about Germany were shared by the then prime minister. Although the majority were optimistic about life with a united Germany, it was clear that considerable concern about German characteristics (almost certainly by Mrs Thatcher) was expressed at the meeting. Some extremely unflattering attributes were mentioned as 'an abiding part of the German character', including 'angst, aggressiveness, assertiveness, bullying, egotism, inferiority complex, sentimentality'.[42]

It was also stated that a tendency to overestimate their own strengths and a capacity to kick over the traces were reasons for misgiving about Germany's future. It was suggested (again probably by Mrs Thatcher) that the way in which the Germans currently used their elbows and threw their weight about in the European Community showed that a lot had still not changed:

> While we all admired and indeed envied what the Germans had achieved in the last 45 years, the fact was that their institutions had not yet been seriously tested by adversity such as a major economic calamity. . . . Could some of the unhappy characteristics of the past reemerge with just as destructive consequences?

One participant at Chequers was right to remind the meeting that Anglo-German antagonism in the twentieth century has been injurious to Europe as a whole and should not be allowed to revive once more. It was entirely legitimate for British cabinet ministers to consider the consequences for Britain and Europe of a united Germany. But the thinking of British politicians in the 1990s ought not to be influenced by outdated prejudice and fear. They should accept that it is not so much a question of the rest of Europe being dominated by an overmighty Germany but of Germany, because of its past and of its present internal preoccupations, being reluctant to pull its weight in the world. A recent German poll revealed that a majority of respondents favour either Switzerland or Sweden as models. Yet enlightened German leadership is essential for the future of the European Community. The British should be understanding and supportive of the stable democracy whose post-war success had already done so much to shape the EC. It is certainly very much in our interests that the close existing links between Britain and Germany should be reinforced by mutual understanding, trust and commitment at both the political and popular levels.

### 'A Rotten Lot'

In a *Times* article on 26 November 1991, Mrs Thatcher's former EC ambassador revealed the truth about her: 'From the beginning,' he wrote, 'in all the innumerable meetings and discussions with her ministers and officials, she shared a deep-seated prejudice against the European Community.' She disliked not only the EC but Europeans in general. Roy Jenkins' diary entry for

22 October 1979 describes a 'wild and whirling interview' with Mrs Thatcher at No 10 when, as president
of the Commission, he was helping prepare the ground
for the Dublin summit whose agenda included a discussion of the British contributions to the EC budget. Mrs
Thatcher launched into an anti-European diatribe:
'They are a rotten lot.'[43] This generally dismissive
attitude is widely shared. Too many Britons simply do
not take the Continentals (with the exception of the
French and Germans) seriously.

Metternich once called Italy 'a geographical
expression'. For many of the British it has been a
marvellous place for a holiday, a cultural tour or a
romantic exile. In the eighteenth century, it was the
Mecca of the Grand Tour, that essential part of a
gentleman's education, containing sightseeing, culture
and good living in varying proportions.[44] Horace Wal-
pole enjoyed carnival time in Florence: 'I have done
nothing but slip out of my domino into bed, and out of
bed into my domino. The end of the carnival is frantic,
bacchanalian.' James Boswell dutifully admired Milan
cathedral and clambered about the ancient ruins of
Rome. However, with his amorous disposition, he
completely ignored Rousseau's advice to him, 'Watch
out for Italian girls – for several reasons'. It was in
Rome that Edward Gibbon got the idea for his master-
piece *The Decline and Fall of the Roman Empire*: 'It
was on the fifteenth of October in the gloom of evening,
as I sat musing on the capitol, while the barefooted
friars were chanting their litanies in the temple of
Jupiter, that I conceived the first thought of my history.'

To Victorian and Edwardian travellers, taking advantage of railways and Cooks tours, Italy became more
accessible. Italy inspired poets like Elizabeth Barrett

Browning and Algernon Charles Swinburne, writers like George Eliot and E. M. Forster and art critics like John Ruskin and John Addington Symonds. Symonds wrote: 'As poets in the truest sense of the word, we English live and breathe through sympathy with the Italians. The magnetic touch which is required to inflame the imagination of the North is derived from Italy.'[45] Yet the art and ruins of Italy were more important to these intellectuals than its people. Elizabeth Barrett Browning, who lived in Florence for many years, knew few Italians socially. Even where there were relationships, these were seldom successful. In E. M. Forster's novel *Where Angels Fear to Tread*, the marriage of Gino and Lilia is doomed: 'No one realised that more than personalities were engaged: that the struggle was national; that generations of ancestors, good, bad or indifferent forbade the Latin man to be chivalrous to the Western woman, the Northern woman to forgive the Latin man.'

There was, however, strong popular backing for Italian unification. The Italian revolutionary, Giuseppe Garibaldi, was a national hero, wildly feted when he visited Britain in 1864. Half a million Londoners lined the streets to cheer him. Fashionable women wore red Garibaldi blouses and red, kepi-shaped Garibaldi hats, while working-class northerners raised money for Garibaldi's guerrilla army. But for all this enthusiasm, for all the fine words of Palmerston, Gladstone and Russell, the British, more concerned about the balance of power and fearful of Continental entanglements, gave little more than moral support to the Italians.

Later, unified Italy disappointed British hopes. Nineteenth-century British statesmen believed it would become a reliable guarantor of the balance of power. The reality was different. Italian leaders from Crispi to

Mussolini, pursued sabre-rattling foreign policies, which usually ended in disaster. It was true that Italy came into the First World War on Britain's side. But Italian intervention came nine months after war first broke out and only after simultaneous negotiations with both sides. In June 1940 the fascist dictator, Benito Mussolini, who had already undermined the traditional Anglo-Italian relationship by his aggression against Ethiopia, declared war on Britain and France when it was clear that France had collapsed. Mussolini's foolish decision brought defeat and dishonour on his unfortunate country.

Post-war, relations between Britain and democratic Italy have been good. But British leaders have tended to underestimate the Italians. They have given too much weight to the instability of Italian governments, the weakness of central institutions and the power of organised crime. They paid insufficient attention to the industrial and technological vitality of modern Italy, so much so that there was a horrified official reaction when the Italians, with some justice, claimed 'il sorpasso', that is, to have overtaken us economically. It is about time the British started understanding how much the Italians have achieved since 1945.

Britain has traditionally has been close to the Benelux countries. In 1585 Elizabeth I sent English troops to aid the Dutch revolt against Phillip II. Though the English and the Dutch fought against each other in the 1660s, in 1688 William of Orange became joint ruler of England with his Stuart wife, Mary. In the war of the Spanish succession, the Dutch Republic fought alongside Britain against the France of Louis XIV. In 1914, Britain's *casus belli* was the German infringement of Belgian neutrality guaranteed by the treaty of 1839 and reasserted by the British in 1870. But, at the outbreak of the Second World War, the Dutch and Belgian refusal to abandon their neutrality, which was in any case cynically flouted by Hitler, undermined their prestige in Britain.

More generally, an unfortunate legacy of the Second World War on British opinion was that Continentals were thought to be unreliable. That was one reason why the British were so negative about plans for European integration. A civil servant, asked to explain British rejection of the Schuman Plan, bluntly summed it up as follows: 'We were being asked to join the Germans, who had started two world wars, the French, who had in 1940 collapsed in the face of German aggression, the Italians, who had changed sides, and the Low Countries, of whom not much was known but who seemed to have put up little resistance to Germany.'[46]

The 'offshore' distrust of mainland Europe, combined with their exceptional historical experience, goes far to explain why the British have been so sceptical about the European Community. Even today, the majority of the British do not consider themselves as European. Despite a gradual shift in opinion, the British, with the Danes, remain the most reluctant Europeans.

# – 3 –

# 'Perfidious Albion'

The British tend to assume that, if no longer predominant in power terms, they are at least morally superior to other European nations. We are, we believe, more democratic, more tolerant and, above all, more trustworthy. As early as 1644, John Milton was arrogantly advising his fellow countrymen: 'Let not England forget her precedence of teaching nations how to live'.[1] But the Continentals have not always seen us as we see ourselves.

While the British give themselves high marks for trustworthiness, others disagree. In July 1990, a Euro-barometer poll, published by the European Commission, showed that, after the Greeks, the British were the most distrusted people in the European Community. This particular finding may have reflected a hostile reaction to Mrs Thatcher's attacks on plans for further European integration. Yet, since joining the European Community, the British have consistently scored badly on the Eurobarometer trust index.

We do not have to accept the estimation of other Europeans. However, if we are to arrive at a balanced view of ourselves and our position in the world, it is worth analysing what they think of us.

### 'Hypocritical' British

Like British attitudes towards the French, French attitudes towards the British are ambivalent, complex and, at least in part, shaped by historic rivalry. On the one hand, the French have a grudging respect for British pragmatism and for the stability of our democratic institutions. On the other hand, they find us difficult to understand, particularly about money, food, class and sex, seldom saying what we think, sometimes even hypocritical. A sympathetic observer, Philippe Daudy, argues that the great British acting and theatrical tradition is both a result of and a relief from our normal reticence:

> The famous impassiveness of the Englishman is a meagre disguise for desire, violence and hatred, or even for shyness and inhibition. But on stage, the alibi of fiction allows him to give way to cries of joy, pain, love or triumph that decency normally forbids.[2]

The French have always been fascinated by British attitudes to sex. A distinguished academic concluded: 'Anyone who has lived long in England knows the bestiality of the majority of the race. . . . The sensuality of the upper classes is concealed by a heavy hypocrisy . . . the lower classes can amuse themselves only grossly and violently.'[3]

The British have had their French admirers. In the eighteenth century, intellectuals like Voltaire and Montesquieu looked across the Channel for inspiration. In his *Lettres philosophiques* (published in 1734), which he wrote after spending two years in England, Voltaire not only popularised the ideas of Newton and Locke but also commented extremely favourably on English values and institutions. He praised our religious tolerance: 'If one religion only were allowed in England, the government would very possibly become arbitrary; if there were but two, the people would cut one another's throats; but as there are thirty, they all live happily and in peace.' He was impressed by the freedom of thought and the relatively open social structure in comparison to the *ancien régime* in France.

Voltaire paid tribute to English parliamentary institutions as established by the 1688 settlement.

> The English are the only people upon earth who have been able to prescribe limits to the power of kings by resisting them; and who, by a series of struggles, have at last established that wise government, where the Prince is all powerful to do good, and at the same time is restrained from committing evil; where the Nobles are great without insolence . . . and where the people share in the government without confusion.

Only in his comments on English literature was Voltaire less than fulsome. He found English poetry undisciplined and lacking classical form and, though he recognised Shakespeare's power and creativity, he dismissed him as having 'not the slightest spark of good taste or the least knowledge of the rules of drama'.

In his *De l'esprit des lois* (published in 1748), in which Montesquieu made his celebrated comparison of different political systems, pride of place was given to the English constitution. Like Voltaire, he had also spent some time in England. English freedom, he concluded, depended on two factors: the substantial 'separation' of executive, legislative and judicial power, and the 'mixture' of monarchy, aristocracy and democracy in Crown, Lords and Commons. Even if Montesquieu's analysis was in part inaccurate, there is little doubt that he considered the English constitution the best available model.

In the nineteenth century, there was French admiration for the new industrial wealth and might of Britain. Among upper-class men, it became fashionable to wear English clothes and take up English leisure pursuits, especially horse-racing. Franglais words entered the French language: for example, *bifteck, fashionable, lunch, dandy, corned beef, pyjama, high life, baby, shirting, cocktail, breakfast, flirt, five o'clock tea, smoking, grill room, lavatory.*[4]

The French went to London. The writer, Villiers de l'Isle Adam, came in search of an heiress. A Parisian marriage broker had kitted him out for the expedition with a fur overcoat, a repeating alarm watch and a new set of false teeth, all to be paid for when he succeeded in catching the heiress. But the heiress rejected him, the broker reclaimed the coat and watch, and 'the discarded suitor was left adrift in London, full of teeth but penniless'.[5] The French literary critic and historian, Hippolyte Taine, whose English pronounciation was so bad that, when he ordered potatoes, he got buttered toast, wondered at the sheer size of the capital: 'Enormous, enormous – this is the word which always recurs. . . . Everything is on a large scale here; the clubs are palaces, the hotels are monuments; the river is an arm of the sea; the cabs go twice as fast . . .'[6]

The English of the Anglophiles were often caricatures. The novelist André Maurois, who was a liaison officer with British troops in France during the First World

War, described stiff-upper-lip public school officers in his *Les Silences du Colonel Bramble*, while, after the Second World War, Pierre Daninos wrote humorously about the adventures in France of the bowler-hatted, umbrella-furled Major Thompson in his *Les Carnet du Major Thompson*.

But if there was an Anglophile strand of opinion, the Anglophobes were more numerous. It was Bishop Bossuet who, in a sermon in 1652, first coined the famous phrase 'la perfide Angleterre',[7] which later became 'La perfide Albion', words bitterly repeated by Napoleon, when, after his defeat at Waterloo and subsequent surrender to the Royal Navy, he was shipped off to the island of St Helena instead of being allowed to stay in England.

There is the other famous remark of Napoleon about the English being a nation of 'boutiquiers'. The conservative thinker, Joseph de Maistre, said in 1814: 'In philosophy, wisdom begins with contempt for English ideas.'[8] My favourite novelist, Stendhal, in his *Souvenirs d'egoisme* wrote: 'The English are, I believe, the most obtuse, most barbaric people in the world. So much so that I forgive them the infamies of Saint Helena. They were not aware of them.' Nineteenth-century commentators like Alphonse Esquiros and Leon Faucher denounced British materialism, inequality and hypocrisy. The French armed forces could not forget that it was the British who were primarily responsible for the defeat of Napoleon at Waterloo, the loss of the first French colonial empire, and the humiliation of Fashoda in 1898, when the French under Marchand were forced by Kitchener to withdraw from Southern Sudan. In 1909, Jeanne d'Arc, burnt at the stake by the English during the Hundred Years War, was beatified by Pope Pius X, following a campaign by the right-wing nationalist movement, *L'Action Française.*

Although the French and the British were allies in the First World War, the collapse of France in June 1940 revived much of the old mistrust. If the British saw the evacuation from Dunkirk as a glorious feat of British arms, for many of the French it was a betrayal by an ally who had, in any case, only made a small contribution to the allied war effort. The British destruction in July 1940 of part of the French fleet at Mers-el-Kebir to prevent it falling into the hands of Hitler added insult to injury. Indeed, the Mers-el-Kebir incident is still remembered as a national humiliation.

Two great Frenchmen represent the Anglophobe and Anglophile traditions – Charles de Gaulle and Jean Monnet. De Gaulle's finest biographer describes him as he arrived in Britain in June 1940 as a confirmed Anglophobe:

Because of family tradition, for his childhood had been marked by the sound of the word Fashoda, uttered around him; because he spoke not English but German; because he had not thought much of the conduct of the British during the 1914–18 war and because he was accustomed to a right wing press – including *L'Action Française* – in which all the misfortunes of French diplomacy had for the last twenty years been put down to the intrigues of perfidious Albion, which the French radicals or socialists 'followed like a dead dog going down the stream'; because he blamed Lord Runciman and Chamberlain for the withdrawal at Munich; and lastly because he thought that Britain's military support of France during the last ten months had been derisory.[9]

De Gaulle was a big enough man to understand that British survival leading to an eventual Anglo-American victory was the only way that France could become free again. Yet, in de Gaulle's view, it was also essential that the Free French gathered around him should be treated not merely as suppliants but as proud representatives of a great nation. De Gaulle wrote in his *Memoires de guerre*: 'It was by acting as the unbending champion of the nation and the state that it might be possible to gather agreement and even enthusiastic support among the French, and to obtain respect and esteem from foreigners.'[10]

It was the 'unbending' national pride of de Gaulle, combined with his visceral mistrust of the British, which led to a series of blazing rows with Churchill, who, despite his fury with de Gaulle, continued (see Chapter 2) to support him throughout the war. Harold Macmillan, who as Churchill's Minister Resident in Algiers had worked closely with de Gaulle, attributed de Gaulle's veto of Macmillan's application to join the Common Market in the early 1960s as in part retribution for his wartime experience: 'If we'd given in to Hitler, we'd have had no trouble with de Gaulle. What they could not forgive us is that we held on, and that we saved France. People can forgive an injury, but they can hardly ever forgive a benefit.'[11] If Macmillan's verdict does less than justice either to de Gaulle's strategic concept of Europe or to the underlying conflict between French and British views on its future, de Gaulle's suspicion of the Anglo-Saxons was certainly a factor in his rejection of Britain.

In contrast, Jean Monnet was a cosmopolitan, as much at home in London or Washington as in Paris. Born and brought up in Cognac, at the age of sixteen he was sent for two years to his father's London agent, a City wine merchant, to learn English. Monnet commented in his memoirs that the French brandy trade had to be on good terms with the Anglo-Saxon world and that the relationship was based not on dependence but on mutual respect: 'At Cognac, one was on equal terms with the British. . . . So we avoided the proud or defensive nationalistic reactions that were beginning to permeate French politics.'[12]

Monnet worked in London throughout the First World War as a key figure in inter-allied purchasing and supply co-ordination. In June 1940 he was again in London as chairman of the Anglo-French Co-ordination Committee. As France collapsed, Monnet proposed an Anglo-French political union by which the two nations would merge. His dramatic plan was taken up by Churchill who, after initial scepticism, backed a Declaration of Union in the hope of persuading the French to fight on. But on 16 June as Churchill prepared to leave for France to persuade the French cabinet, Pétain formed a new government and within a few hours asked the Germans for an armistice. Monnet's idea of Anglo-French Union was stillborn.

After the war, Monnet was always strongly in favour of British participation in plans for European integration. However, he refused to accept that the British should have a veto on progress. In June 1950, in a discussion with Stafford Cripps, then chancellor of the exchequer, about the Schuman Plan, he said: 'I hope with all my heart that you will join in this from the start. But if you don't, we shall go ahead without you.

And I'm sure that, because you are realists, you will adjust to the facts when you see that we have succeeded.'[13] When Britain applied to join the Common Market in the early 1960s, Monnet strongly supported British membership. As he put it,

> Europe . . . needs the qualities that reside in the British people. . . . The British have a better understanding than the continentals of institutions and how to use them. Continentals tend to believe that problems are solved by men. Undoubtedly, men are important; but without institutions they reach no great and enduring decisions. This the British have long understood. That is why, unlike many people, I had no fear that their accession would upset the working of the Community.[14]

Monnet's optimism about the British was not justified by British behaviour in the Community. During the 1980s, old French prejudices about the British were also fuelled by Mrs Thatcher's strained relations with successive French presidents (see Chapter 2) and her hostile attitude to European integration. Distrust between the British and French sometimes led to absurd incidents.

The row over an interview with Edith Cresson, then Socialist prime minister, which appeared in *The Observer* on 18 June 1991 was a classic example of French mistrust (and misunderstanding) of the British. Four years before, Edith Cresson, when out of power, had given an interview to the millionaire publisher, Naim Attallah, for a book on women in which she gave forthright views on the role of women, politics and sex. In answer to Attallah's comment that in Anglo-Saxon countries most men preferred the company of other men, Madame Cresson somewhat unwisely replied that a quarter of men in England were homosexuals: 'I remember from strolling about in London – and girls still make the same observation – the men don't look at you. ... A man who isn't interested in women is in some way a little maimed.' *The Observer*, in what its correspondent John Sweeney described as 'a perfectly straightforward piece of good, mischief-making journalism', chose to publish this interview only after Edith Cresson had become prime minister. *The Sun* followed up *The Observer* story with a typical headline: 'Brits blast poofter jibe from Mrs Frog'. The reaction from the Cresson office in Paris was understandably furious. Jean-Phillipe Atger, in charge of press relations, exploded: 'We would never do a thing like this. ... It is always the English that play these games. Always Great Britain.' John Sweeney wrote that Atger pronounced Great Britain as if it were 'not a country but a particularly nasty form of sheep apoplexy'.[15]

But if the French continued to find us irritating, they have at least had the consolation that the relationship with the British was no longer of the first importance. As a Continental nation, the French have always had to look in a number of directions; south to the Pyrénnées and Spain; south-east to the Alps and Italy and Switzerland; east to the Rhine and Germany; north to the Low Countries; and north-west to the Channel and Britain. After three disastrous wars, French political leaders came to the conclusion that the overriding objective of French foreign policy had to be reconciliation with Germany. Hence the 1950 Schuman Declaration, De Gaulle's historic agreement with Adenauer in 1963, the close relationship between Giscard and Schmidt in the 1970s and between Mitterrand and Kohl in the 1980s, Mrs Thatcher's histrionics were more a tiresome distraction than central to French concerns. The Paris–Bonn axis has been the link that has mattered.

However, in the Europe of the 1990s, with a more powerful unified Germany, it may be that the French will be looking for a closer relationship with the British, not so much as an alternative to the Franco-German alliance, but as a prudent addition to it. A British government with a positive approach to the European Community might then find it will become possible to create a new *entente cordiale*.

### 'Backward' Britain

The Germans respect our parliament and our commitment to democratic values and 'fair play'. But they are appalled by our industrial backwardness and inefficiency, find some of our institutions, particularly our class system, anachronistic and cannot accept the insular rejection of European integration by our political leaders. At a popular level our traditional reputation for good manners (not always well deserved) has been undermined by the behaviour of English soccer hooligans and holiday 'lager louts'.

As was described in the previous chapters, relations between the northern German states and Hanoverian Britain were close. As a young man, Frederick the Great of Prussia had hoped to carry out his Hanoverian mother's wish and marry George II's second daughter, Amelia, but the ploy had been vetoed by his hated father, Frederick William. Frederick remained friendly with successive British envoys in Berlin and even received gifts of money from George II to pay off his personal debts. As his long and intimate relationship with Voltaire demonstrates, he greatly admired French culture. But politically he became Britain's main Continental ally. The large-scale and sustained British subsidy helped him to stay in the Seven Years War when his armies were encircled by the formidable Franco-Austro-Russian alliance. In the book which he wrote at the end of his life for his nephew his advice was not to start another war but instead to persuade Britain to pay Prussia to keep out of one.

In the nineteenth century, liberal Germans admired the industrial might and parliamentary institutions of Britain. Particularly in northern cities like Hamburg, the middle classes imitated English fashions: 'the Tudor-style spread "like a plague"; one played whist in a drawing-room full of English furniture, on the walls of which hung coloured lithographs of London scenes, or strolled in one's "English-landscape" garden.'[16] The conservative upper classes were also enthusiastic about 'der englische lebenstil' by which they meant men's clothes, London clubs, weekends in the country, and horse-racing and shooting. To live like an 'English gentleman' was all the rage. When Crown Prince Frederick of Prussia married Princess Victoria of England in 1856, Berlin went wild.

But some Germans had become disillusioned with the British. The poet Heinrich Heine, complained:

> Whenever I talk with Englishmen about my fatherland, I notice with deep humiliation that the hate they feel for the French is more honourable to the latter than the impertinent affection which they bestow upon us Germans. . . . They love us because of our maritime weakness which prevents

any fear of commercial rivalry. They love us because of our political naiveté which they hope to exploit in the old way in case of a war with France.[17]

Nationalists were dismayed by the failure of Britain to give practical support to the cause of German unification. The British had opposed the Zollverein, the customs union which had protected German industry. They had been on the side of Denmark in 1864 and backed Austria in 1866. Although neutral in the Franco-Prussia war, they had supplied French ships with ammunition to blockade German ports. In his *History of Germany in the Nineteenth Century*, Heinrich von Treitschke denounced 'the most sacred principle of the British, the principle that England alone is entitled to deceive other powers'.[18] Bismarck encouraged anti-British feeling for his own political ends, though he did not share it. He loved Shakespeare, Byron and Scott. He admired Britain for having fought for and won imperial supremacy. But, given British isolationism, he did not believe that she would be a reliable ally. Had not Frederick the Great been shamefully deserted by George III and his leading minister, Lord Bute, at the end of the Seven Years War? In any case, Victorian Britain could usually be ignored. In 1865, he quipped: 'The thunders of Albion are no longer backed by lightning charges; even children do not fear them.'

When at the end of the nineteenth century, imperial Germany, under Kaiser William II, sought to secure an overseas empire, it found the British response hypocritical. Had not the British carved out an empire for themselves? Why should they try and stop the Germans doing the same? It was Churchill himself who admitted:

'We have got all we want in territory, and our claim to be left in unmolested enjoyment of vast and splendid possessions, mainly acquired by violence, largely maintained by force, often seems less reasonable to others than to us.'[19]

To German eyes, Britain's attitude to Germany was irrational. In 1914, Bethmann Hollweg, the German chancellor, in an emotional farewell to the British ambassador, blamed the British for the outbreak of the war: 'It was in London's hand to curb French revanchism and Pan Slav chauvinism. It has not done so, but has, rather, repeatedly egged them on. And now England has actively helped them.'[20]

Traditional feelings of friendship were eclipsed by war. Admiral von Tirpitz, the architect of Germany's naval expansion which had so upset the British, gave vent to his fury against Britain: 'England, with brutal egoism, recognises only Englishmen. Niggers and Germans are on the same level to them. Never has the world been so terrorised as by this pirate people on their island. Only force can help against them.'[21] When their war leaders argued that Britain was the main enemy, the German people, influenced by the hardships imposed by the allied naval blockade, believed them. At the front, however, German soldiers, mirroring the British soldiers' view of the Germans, were inclined to admire the fighting qualities of the British 'Tommies'.

In what the German historian, Golo Mann, has called 'the darkest chapter' of German history from 1933–45, the Germans allowed themselves to be led by an evil adventurer into another world war, once again with Britain as a prominent opponent.[22] Hitler may have thought he could do a deal with Britain whereby Germany agreed not to challenge Britain's imperial role in return for a free hand on the Continent. But not even the most fervent British appeaser could agree to abandon the whole of central and Eastern Europe, let alone France, to their fate. Given Hitler's aims, renewed Anglo-German conflict was inevitable.

How far did the German people come to hate the British? Christabel Bielenberg, an Englishwoman married to a German lawyer who spent the war in Germany, wrote in her autobiography: 'Goebbels never succeeded in making the Germans hate. . . . The Germans had not risen and torn the airmen to bits who were killing so indiscriminately night after night. I had never heard a cheer go up when an allied bomber came crashing down in flames'.[23] She gave a moving account of the humanity of the Black Forest villagers who sheltered her and her children for the last two years of the war. Christabel Bielenberg's conclusion, however, was that, after years of Nazi rule, the Germans 'had become an ignorant demoralized insensate mass and I could only be grateful to the few who had shone out reassuringly like beacons'. She was referring to the unsuccessful German resistance – soldiers like Claus von Stauffenberg and Henning von Tresckow, Social Democrat leaders like Julius Leber and Carl Mierendorf, aristocrats like Helmut von Moltke and Adam von Trott – all of whom paid for failure with their lives.

After the war, the British contribution to building German democracy (described in Chapter 2) was, on the whole, appreciated by German politicians, particularly by Social Democrats, some of whom, for example Willi Eichler, Erich Ollenauer and Richard Löwenthal, had spent the war as exiles in London. But it was the Christian Democrats, led by Konrad Adenauer, who dominated the early years of the Federal Republic.

Unfortunately, Adenauer had suffered a bad experience at the hands of the British. In October 1945, a British brigadier, acting on the orders of the British military government, sacked Konrad Adenauer as Mayor of Cologne (which the Americans had appointed him six months before). In 1933, Adenauer, then a prominent member of the Catholic centre party, had also been sacked by Hitler from the same post for refusing to meet him or to allow Nazi swastika flags to be flown from the main city bridge in his honour. In 1945 the British apparently did not like Adenauer's requests for more coal and building materials for his city and were infuriated when he refused to cut down trees in the city park for use as firewood. Adenauer argued that the people of Cologne could get through one cold winter but that it took at least fifteen years to grow good trees. According to his own account, Adenauer was marched into the brigadier's office and kept standing while told of his dismissal. Adenauer never forgave the British but his dismissal launched him belatedly on a national political career. As chancellor, Adenauer, a Rhinelander who spoke French well, put all his weight and influence behind a Franco-German reconciliation.

The 1960s were a watershed in post-war Anglo-German relations. Before 1960, Germany had to some extent been learning from Britain. After 1960, it was Germany which forged ahead, particularly economically. Germany backed the British application for membership of the Common Market. But it was the support of a more important for a less important partner. German political leaders, including Schmidt and Brandt as well as Adenauer, also made it quite clear that the French relationship came first. During the 1970s, Germans

began expressing their impatience with what they saw
as the British failure to tackle their own industrial and
economic problems and their disappointment with Britain as a member of the EC.

The Anglo-German Königswinter conference, the
brainchild of a formidable Anglophile, Frau Lilo Mil-
chsack, is a gathering of British and German politicians,
journalists, diplomats, academics, bankers, industrial-
ists and trade unionists which has been meeting for over
forty years. As such, it provides a unique vantage point
from which to view the attitude of the German liberal
establishment towards Britain. The overwhelming
impression is one of regret and frustration that the
British have proved to be such reluctant Europeans.
The criticism of Theo Sommer, distinguished editor
of *Die Zeit*, is typical:

> Successive Labour and Conservative governments
> have exposed us to constant bickering about Brit-
> ain's financial contribution. We have seen an oil-
> giddy Britain blocking a Common European
> energy policy; a Britain emulating de Gaulle's
> empty chair tactics when it came to determing the
> value of the 'Green Pound'; a Britain foiling the
> Community's efforts towards establishing a
> common fisheries policy; a Britain being difficult
> about electing the European parliament; a Britain
> cold shouldering the European Monetary System;
> a Conservative Prime Minister raising the wild
> spectre of 'identikit Europeans' to block progress
> towards 'a more perfect union' . . . a Britain which,
> in the words of *The Sunday Times*, behaved all too
> often like a man who joins a club, imbibes cheer-
> fully at the bar every evening but is curiously

absent each time when it is his turn to stand a round of drinks.

In 1978, I listened to Richard von Weizsäcker, later to become Federal president, warning that Britain's German friends were 'worried, disappointed and shocked' by our negative and self-centred conduct as a member of the European Community. Ten years later, I even heard the former chancellor, Helmut Schmidt, growling like a fierce old lion that de Gaulle had been right all along about the British and the European Community.[24]

The Germans were particularly upset by Mrs Thatcher's boorish behaviour. In 1980, at the 30th anniversary meeting at St Catherine's, Cambridge, Mrs Thatcher gave a dinner for the Federal chancellor, Helmut Schmidt. She spent much of her after-dinner speech bitterly upbraiding the Germans about the British financial contribution. Schmidt, who had attended sixteen out of thirty Königswinter meetings and had expected a more statesmanlike approach, was clearly much annoyed by Mrs Thatcher's tone, a feeling which was shared by all the Germans present (and most of the British). In 1990, the year of German reunification, Mrs Thatcher gave a 40th anniversary dinner for another Federal chancellor, Helmut Kohl. Once again, Mrs Thatcher totally misjudged the occasion. In her speech she gave no hint that she understood the historic significance of German reunification or had any kind of vision of Europe's future. It was noticeable that Mrs Thatcher and Chancellor Kohl hardly addressed a single word to each other during dinner. However, Mrs Thatcher was overheard loudly telling the German ambassador that it would take another forty years before the British would trust the Germans, a remark which obviously did not go down well with her guests.

The former Social Democrat (SPD) chancellor, Helmut Schmidt, whose home is in the traditionally Anglophile city of Hamburg, once told the British journalist, Peter Jenkins, that Britain was 'an underdeveloped country'. I asked an SPD friend who knows Britain well to sum up his views of the British. He said that he found us, in many respects, backward and out of date. He despised our class structure and snobbery, found our education system appalling and thought our state structure was far too centralised. While Germany was 'high tech', Britain was 'low tech'. Above all, the British were still too nationalistic and did not yet understand the need to be European.

Yet, despite their disappointment with Britain in the EC, many Germans believe that there is a strong case for a close relationship between Germany and Britain to supplement rather than replace the existing Franco-German alliance. In their view 'An active triangle in the EC, Germany, France and Great Britain' would not only lessen Germany's political dependence on France but also give a better balance to the European Community.[25]


**'Bad Europeans'**
Other Continental nations, such as the Italians, the Dutch and the Belgians, have traditionally had an admiration for the British. They strongly supported British membership of the European Community and were bitterly disappointed first by our refusal to join and then by our reluctance to participate wholeheartedly in its development. In their eyes, the British are too often 'bad Europeans'.

In the nineteenth century, Italian nationalists looked to Britain. The Italian statesman, Camillo Cavour, was a fervent admirer of Britain. As a young man, he learnt English by getting up at 4 a.m. to read Adam Smith. He studied farming methods, was converted to the Utilitarianism of Jeremy Bentham, and was impressed by Conservative politicians like Robert Peel. On a visit to Britain, he concluded: 'The English have learnt how to work together; they know how to discuss without altercation and to respect individual opinions.'[26] However, despite his respect for the British, Cavour always believed that the support of the French was far more valuable than British public opinion. Napoleon III had gone to war for the Italian cause, while Britain had only given moral support. 'If England had wished to give us effective help, if she still wished to give it, she would guarantee, quite cheaply, the independence of Europe. Unfortunately, her platonic sympathies are not enough.'[27]

Liberal Victorian Britain, however, was a haven for Italian as well as other European political exiles (including Karl Marx and Louis Napoleon). After the abortive radical uprising of 1821 in Piedmont, my great-great-grandfather, Evasio Radice, one of the ring leaders, eventually escaped to Britain where he was fortunate enough to become a university professor, even though he was condemned to death (and hung in effigy) by the reactionary Piedmontese authorities, acting under threat from Austria. Later he returned to become a member of the first Piedmontese parliament and an ambassador to the short-lived German parliament in Frankfurt. But he remained very grateful to the nation which had befriended him and always spoke of Britain as 'this great country', a view shared by most Italians. Giving political asylum is a traditional 'Victorian value' which the British should not abandon.

Like the French, the Italian upper classes aped English fashions. The men bought English suits and shoes. Some even sent their shirts to London to be laundered and ironed. Luigi Barzini, an acute observer of national foibles, tells of an Italian count who went to London accompanied by his manservant. He sent him out the first morning to see how the natives were dressed. His servant came back perplexed 'Signor conto,' he said, 'there's nobody in London dressed like an Englishman except you and me.' Barzini also remembers the Victorian porcelain toilet bowl, a 'must' in Italian country houses: 'The English water-closet bowl of my childhood proudly bore the name "Favoria" and the arms of the United Kingdom, "Dieu et Mon Droit," lion and unicorn and all, exactly where one had to direct one's stream.'[28]

The Anglophile tradition survived Mussolini's fascist regime. Many British accounts pay tribute to the brave and generous help give by Italian peasants to escaped British prisoners of war in 1943–4. 'They hid us, escorted us, gave us money, clothes and food . . . all the time taking tremendous risks. . . . We English owe a great debt of gratitude to those Italians whose help alone made it possible for us to live, and finally to escape.'[29]

After the war, the Italians looked to Britain to be a leader of Europe. In 1955 Gaetano Martino, the Italian foreign minister, invited the British to be present at the Messina Conference which led to the establishment of the Common Market. The Italians strongly supported the British application for membership because they believed that Britain would act as a balancing force to

France and Germany and, unlike de Gaulle, saw the British relationship with Washington as potentially valuable to the European Community.

They have, however, been much disappointed by British membership. The Italians are amongst the most enthusiastic supporters of European integration. Gianni de Michelis, then Italian foreign minister, explained the reasons why to a British journalist in June 1990: 'The European process is associated with personal prosperity for Italians, and with the promise that Europe would help Italy to improve bureaucratic efficiency.'[30] Given this enthusiasm, it is not surprising that they have been shocked by Britain's negative attitude, especially when Mrs Thatcher was in power. Twice Italian political leaders got their own back by inflicting a humiliating reverse on Mrs Thatcher.

On the first occasion, at the Milan summit of June 1985, it was the Italian prime minister, Bettino Craxi, who called a vote under Article 236 of the Rome Treaty to set up an intergovernmental conference. This vote put the British in a seven to three minority and led to the Single European Act which authorised qualified majority voting and led to the pressure for economic and monetary union. On the second occasion, in October 1990, the Italian EC presidency, under Giulio Andreotti, called a special summit in Rome which, against Mrs Thatcher's wishes, committed the EC to the objective of a single currency and to a staged approach to its achievement (with the second stage beginning on 1 January 1994 and a report on the workings of the second stage within these years). It was Andreotti's coup in Rome which was the cause of Mrs Thatcher's astonishing behaviour, first at her press conference and later during her European Council statement to the

House of Commons. It was these outbursts which led to Sir Geoffrey Howe's resignation and thus indirectly to Mrs Thatcher's defeat and resignation in November 1990.

As was outlined in the last chapter, the Benelux countries have historically looked to Britain for protection. With the exception of the Anglo-Dutch wars of the 1660s, from the 1585 Treaty of Nonsuch through to the August 1914 declaration of war against Germany over the issue of Belgian neutrality, there have always been close links between the peoples of the Low Countries and the British.

During the Second World War, the Dutch and Belgian governments in exile were stationed in London. After the war, they counted on British leadership to unite Europe. In 1941, Paul-Henri Spaak, the great Belgian statesman, presciently warned the Conservative MP, Irene Ward:

> After the war Europe will be glad to unite behind Britain's victorious leadership. . . . She must herself assume the responsibilities born of her supremacy. If Britain fails to recognize her duty to Europe, if she does not present a continental policy which makes her a strong leader in Europe, she must expect to be rapidly deprived of the fruits of her present efforts.[31]

The Benelux countries supported British involvement in both the Schuman Plan and the Common Market and backed Britain's subsequent application for EC membership. They were, however, disappointed by the reluctance of the British to join and by the scepticism which this displayed once they had joined.

In May 1977, Roy Jenkins, the new president of the European Commission, went to Luxemburg to see Gaston Thorn, the Luxemburg prime minister and former president of the Commisison. Thorn told Jenkins that the sense of disillusion with the British was considerable.

Perhaps unfairly, they put up with things from the French they wouldn't put up with from the British because they were used to the French and they were used to playing a tiresome game with them, and they could have one country doing this but they could not have two. Furthermore, they had thought that when the British came in, while we would not bring great economic strength or wealth we would bring a democratic infusion, and therefore our hesitancy over direct elections was a mystifying disappointment. And they had also thought that we would bring not so much a sense of efficiency, but a sense of fair play to our chairing of the various Councils, and therefore our handling of the Agricultural Council and of the Research Council had also been damaging.[32]

The Benelux countries remain friendly towards the British. But they are enthusiastic supporters of European integration. Belgian politicians, already involved in running a federal Belgium, generally support the idea of more power going 'up' to the EC and 'down' to the regions, while for the Dutch a federal Europe offers a defence against being dominated by the larger nations. That is why they find British scepticism about Europe hard to stomach.

After the war, British prestige on the Continent was

extremely high. Now nearly fifty years later, much of it has been dissipated. Partly, it is because of the decline in our economic and political power. The main reason is, however, because we are thought to be 'bad Europeans'. At the beginning, we not only declined to join but even sabotaged schemes for European unity. When we eventually joined, we carped, criticised, and made little positive contribution. Britain has been a great disappointment to its European friends.

# – 4 –

# Missing European Boats

At one stage during the negotiations leading up to the crucial December 1991 European Council meeting at Maastricht, the president of the EC Commission, Jacques Delors, reminded Douglas Hurd, the British foreign secretary, that Britain had once before misunderstood its European neighbours when it failed to join the founding six EC states in negotiating the Treaty of Rome in 1957. He quoted a story of the British representative at the Messina talks announcing that he was happy to be leaving 'because you are not going to agree on anything, and if you do agree anything it will never happen and if it does happen it will be a disaster'. The Delors version is almost certainly apocryphal, though, when the Schuman Plan was announced by the Six in June 1950, the British ambassador, Sir Oliver Harvey, issued a statement which said that there had been international organisations set up before 'with fanfares of trumpets which encounter only difficulties and disappointments when the time comes to put them into practice'.[1]

However, even if his story about Messina is unsubstantiated, Delors is basically right. The history of British policy towards European integration both before and after Britain joined the European Community, is a sorry tale of missed opportunities. After the war, the leadership of Europe was Britain's for the asking. The prestige of Britain, as one of the victors, had never been higher. The defeated and devastated countries of Europe looked to Britain to provide the guidance necessary to construct a new post-war order which would unite Europe as never before. But the British, who still believed in their world role and who were in any case sceptical about the Continental Europeans, preferred to remain detached. Even when Britain joined the EC, it remained reluctant and ambivalent, a posture which minimised its influence on its EC partners and on the direction of the EC. Britain's European policy has been a classic case of 'too little and too late'. The pattern is one of initial British rejection of European advances, followed by British attempts either to create an alternative, looser model or to stand aloof, culminating, after a period of time, in a British acceptance on Continental terms of the original plan. The only fair verdict is that it adds up to political failure on a grand scale.

### 'The Durham Miners Won't Wear It'

It would be wrong to describe the great reforming Labour administrations of 1945–51, led by Clement Attlee, as simply anti-European. The formidable British foreign secretary, Ernest Bevin, was closely involved in three developments which had a dramatic impact on the shape of post-war Europe. It was his prompt response to the historic speech by General George Marshall, the American secretary of state, offering economic aid to Europe, which led to the setting up of the Organisation of European Economic Cooperation (OEEC) and the successful implementation of the Marshall Plan. Similarly, Bevin, responding to the communist coup in Czechoslovakia in February 1948, was the architect of the Brussels Treaty, which united Britain with France and the three Benelux countries in a defensive alliance. Last but not least, he was also at least in part responsible for the creation in April 1949 of the North Atlantic Treaty Organisation by which the United States became directly involved in the defence of Western Europe.

But if Labour leaders saw it as a British interest to preserve the security and to promote the recovery of Western Europe (including the rehabilitation of Germany), they wished to do it on the basis of co-operation between nation states. They rejected any idea of British participation in European institutions in which there was a pooling of sovereignty. They were also concerned about being too intimately involved with Europe. Bevin saw British post-war foreign policy in terms of three priorities: the relationship with the United States, so vital to national security; the Commonwealth and overseas territories so important in terms of tradition and prestige; and the relationship with Europe. Of these, the relationship with Europe ranked the lowest. To Bevin, too close an involvement with plans for greater European unity was bound to be at the expense of Britain's special relationship with the United States and her world role as leader of the Commonwealth.

The first crucial test of British intentions came with the Schuman Plan. This plan was the brainchild of Jean Monnet, who has been described as having 'done more to unite Europe on a permanent basis than all the emperors, kings, generals and dictators since the fall of the Roman empire'.[2] Monnet, who was then head of the

French Planning Commission, had first approached his British counterpart, Sir Edwin Plowden, in April 1949 to find out whether Anglo-French economic co-operation could provide the basis for European unity. Only after being politely but firmly rebuffed by the British did he turn to Konrad Adenauer and the West Germans.

Monnet's idea was to pool French and German coal and steel resources under one supranational authority. He hoped that joint control of these two vital industries would not only guarantee peace between the two countries but also become 'the germ of European unity'.[3] He persuaded the French foreign minister, Robert Schuman, to adopt the plan as his own. On 9 May 1950, Schuman, with the backing of the French and West German cabinets, put forward proposals for an international authority to regulate the coal and steel production of France and Germany and of any other country which might wish to participate.

The announcement of the plan presented the British Labour government with a dilemma. On the one hand, they did not wish to appear to oppose such a bold and imaginative attempt to end the old conflict between France and Germany. Hence Attlee's welcome for the French initiative in the House of Commons. On the other hand, there was a general consensus by ministers and officials that British participation in the plan as it stood would involve an unacceptable loss of sovereignty. It was, therefore, decided to seek negotiations but without accepting the principle of ceding control to a supranational authority.

Despite some initial wavering, the French and Germans refused to accept the British attempt at dilution. On 1 June, Schuman handed the British ambassador a virtual ultimatum: either the British accepted the principle of ceding sovereignty by 7 p.m. the next day or they would be excluded from the negotiations. A hastily arranged British cabinet meeting under Herbert Morrison's chairmanship (Attlee was on holiday and Bevin ill in hospital) rejected the French ultimatum. As a result, the British stood aloof from the first successful attempt at European integration. France, Germany, Italy, Holland, Belgium and Luxemburg went ahead and set up the European Coal and Steel Community the following April. Dean Acheson, the American secretary of state at that time, rightly called the British decision 'the greatest mistake of the post-war period'.[4] Britain had lost the initiative in Europe. However, in the circumstances of the time and given the prevailing attitudes of the British and their political leaders, both Labour and Conservative, there was never much chance that any British government would have agreed to join a supranational European organisation. Herbert Morrison's reaction to the Schuman ultimatum is revealing of the prevailing cast of mind. Tracked down by Kenneth Younger, minister of state at the Foreign Office, and by Sir Edwin Plowden, Morrison listened to an explanation of what the plan involved in a passage at the back of the Ivy restaurant where he was having supper after the theatre. Pausing for a moment, he said: 'It's no good. We can't do it: the Durham miners won't wear it.'[5] In other words, Morrison believed that the miners, having recently achieved the nationalisation of the coal industry, would not agree to putting British pits under the control of a European authority.

Other motives were equally important. There was the special relationship with the United States. Despite the fact that, by 1950, the Americans were already urging us to play a more active role in Europe, the maintenance of the relationship with the United States was, according to the Foreign Office 'paramount'.[6] The British fear, perhaps an understandable one at the height of the cold war, was that, if they committed themselves too closely to Europe, the United States might be tempted to return to its old isolationist ways.

There was also the strong feeling (described in Chapter 2) that the mainland European countries were politically unstable and economically shaky. The official Labour Party statement 'European Unity', drafted by Denis Healey, then international secretary, but toughened up by the chairman of the International Committee, Hugh Dalton, who was fiercely anti-German, uncompromisingly rejected the Schuman Plan as the thin edge of the federalist wedge.[7] But it contained two sentences which gave the game away. 'In every respect except distance we are closer to our kinsmen in Australia and New Zealand than we are to Europe. We are closer in language and in origins, in social habits and institutions, in political outlook and in economic interest.' The implication was that the British Labour government should not put at risk the Commonwealth nor the recently created welfare state for the sake of unreliable Continentals, especially when some of the most influential European leaders appeared to be Catholic right wingers like Adenauer, Schuman and de Gasperi and too many of the socialists still seemed to be prisoners of their Marxist past.

Jean Monnet shrewdly summed up the difference between the British and the Continentals' attitude to European integration in the following terms:

With the exception of the UK and the other neutrals every country in Western Europe has been defeated in war and every country has been occupied by an enemy army of occupation. So we are disillusioned with our institutions and are ready for change and a new approach. You are not.[8]

## 'Bored' with Europe

The British were fortunate enough to be given another chance in 1955 when they were invited to be a founder member of the Common Market. Once again, they turned down an opportunity, perhaps the last real one, of taking the lead in Europe.

The drive for a European Common Market was launched by the foreign ministers of Belgium, France, the Federal Republic, Italy, Luxemburg and the Netherlands at the Messina Conference in June 1955. The then Belgian foreign minister, the distinguished European statesman, Paul-Henri Spaak, described the conclusion of Messina in his memoirs: 'On the last day of the Conference we had to work through the night, drafting the final communiqué. The sun was rising over Mount Etna as we were returning to our rooms, tired but happy. Far reaching decisions had been taken.'[9] The inspiration for the Common Market idea had come from the Benelux countries whose own customs union (established in 1947) had already proved highly successful. Following Messina, Spaak was given the responsibility of producing a detailed plan of action. The 'Spaak' report was unanimously accepted at the Venice Conference in April 1956 and subsequently provided the inspiration for the Treaty of Rome, signed by the Six in March 1957.

The British government, by then a Conservative one, was asked to participate in this far-reaching development. In opposition in the 1940s, the Conservatives had appeared more favourable to European integration than the Labour Party. As was described in Chapter 1, in September 1946 Winston Churchill made an eloquent speech at Zurich calling for European unity. He attended the Congress of the European Movement at the Hague and played a prominent part in the Council of Europe, set up in 1949. But once he was returned to power in 1951, it became clear that the Conservative government led by Churchill was no more enthusiastic about European integration than its Labour predecessor. It rejected the Schuman Plan and refused to support British involvement in the project for a European army which Churchill called a 'sludgy amalgam'. Like its Labour predecessor, it gave a much higher priority to Britain's world role, to the Commonwealth and the colonies, and to the special relationship with the United States than to European integration.

It was symptomatic of the Conservative government's attitude that, while other countries were represented at Messina by their foreign ministers, Britain, on the express instructions of Anthony Eden, who had succeeded Churchill as prime minister, sent a middle-ranking civil servant, an under secretary at the Board of Trade, and then only as an observer. The luckless bureaucrat, Russell Bretherton, was also deputed to attend the subsequent Spaak Committee meetings in Brussels.

Paul-Henri Spaak characterised Bretherton's tactics as follows:

Throughout our early discussions his attitude was one of distinct scepticism. While the representatives of the other powers went about their work with a will, he remained silent for the most part. When he did join in our discussions it was only to express doubt as to whether his country would accept whatever idea looked liked becoming the basis of agreement at any given time. This wait and see attitude of his persisted until the decisive conference, held in Venice in April 1956. When we resumed our work in Brussels, the British observer was nowhere to be seen. His government did not try too hard to explain, let alone justify, his absence. The fact of the matter was that the British were not yet ready to take part in our European venture.[10]

The British were certainly not ready. Eden, though he was a great admirer of French culture, was a convinced Atlanticist. Significantly he scarcely mentioned the Messina Conference in his memoirs. He was far more concerned with Britain's relationship with the United States, the threat to Britain's position in the Middle East and relations with the Soviet Union. He was also a strong imperialist and believed in the Commonwealth. He once said, 'If you looked at the postbag of any English village . . . ninety per cent (of the letters from abroad) would come from way beyond Europe.' With respect to a closer integration with Europe, his comment was that 'we know in our bones we cannot do it'.

R. A. Butler, the chancellor of the exchequer, a man with a strong imperialist and Indian background, dismissed the personal pleas of the Dutch and Belgian foreign ministers, both extremely anxious to secure the involvement of their traditional ally in the Common Market project, with studied indifference. He considered that Beyen, the Dutch foreign minister, was 'very pushing' for a representative of such a small country and found Spaak's enthusiasm incomprehensible. Spaak commented on his meeting with Butler: 'I don't think I could have shocked him more when I tried to appeal to his imagination than if I would have taken my trousers off.'[11]

In his retirement, Butler deeply regretted his failure to understand the importance of Messina. He admitted that the decision not to take part in the detailed negotiations following Messina was not even discussed at cabinet level, so confident were Eden and Butler that the European Common Market would not get off the ground. He summed up the British attitude in one word: 'Boredom'.[12]

The government's failure to understand what was happening on the Continent cost Britain dear. There is little doubt that, if Britain had been involved in the European Community at the beginning, its rules, particularly as regards agriculture, would have been far more favourable to British interests. The British could also have achieved a better deal for the Commonwealth. But because of their lack of foresight and vision, the British government missed the last opportunity of creating a European Community at least partially in their own image.

## Late Entry

At the beginning of the 1960s, after a futile effort to create a loose free trade area as an alternative to the EC, the Conservative government, now led by Harold Macmillan, who was more European-minded than Eden, decided to take the plunge and apply for member-

ship of the Common Market. Jean Monnet had rightly
predicted that Britain would only make the fundamental
shift in its policy towards the Continent when it was
seen that the new European Community was successful.
There were two other powerful factors which pushed
the government towards a policy reappraisal. Firstly,
there was a growing awareness, following the 1956
Suez débâcle, of the decline in British power. Secondly,
the disturbing signs of relative economic weakness,
especially compared to Germany and France, were also
increasingly recognised, particularly by the civil service
establishment. After an official review (chaired by the
head of the treasury, Sir Frank Lee) which concluded
that there were strong political and economic arguments
for joining the Common Market, Macmillan announced
to the Commons in July 1961 the historic decision that
Britain was applying for entry. In his subsequent Commons speech, he played down the sovereignty issue. The
EEC was an economic and not a political community,
he argued. Entry would be advantageous to British
industry ('a bracing cold shower' he told the Conservative Conference in October). It would also help unite
the Continent and give Britain a new role of leadership
in Europe. 'I believe that our right place is in the
vanguard of the movement towards the greater unity of
the world, and we can lead better from within rather
than outside,'[13] he proclaimed to MPs.

The tragedy for the British government was that it
had left its application too late. With the accession to
power in 1958 of de Gaulle, the western half of the
European Continent was now being organised against
Britain. As has been described in Chapters 2 and 3, de
Gaulle's idea of Europe did not include Britain. It is no
coincidence that, a week after his devastating press

conference in January 1963 at which he announced that Britain was not ready for EC membership, he signed a treaty of friendship with the Federal Republic. Taken together with the veto on British membership, it was a clear signal that, while de Gaulle remained in power, the European Community would be run by a Franco-German duumvirate rather than an Anglo-French-German triumvirate. De Gaulle's view that the European Community ought to be a 'Europe des États' may have had more in common with the one held by most British politicians than that of the Germans. But, without the British, it was easier for the French both to play a leading role within the Community and also to ensure that its development was broadly in line with French interests.

By 1970 when the Heath government reopened negotiations for entry (de Gaulle had resigned in 1969), the direction of the European Community had already been shaped by a historic compromise between the French and Germans. For the Germans, the political reward for accepting French leadership in Europe was the respectability that the French-German relationship brought with it. German industry gained access to the markets of the other member states, while French farmers were protected by the Common Agricultural Policy (CAP). For these benefits, the Germans were prepared to become the main paymasters of the Community.

But the Franco-German bargain was bound to create difficulties for the British. The combination of a budget mostly devoted to the CAP *and* the method of budget funding agreed on the eve of the Heath negotiations (based on the receipts from a common external tariff on industrial goods, levies on imported goods and up to 1 per cent of national VAT resources) meant that Britain faced the prospect of becoming, after the Federal Republic, the EC's largest net contributor.

However, Edward Heath, a dedicated European who had spoken in favour of the Schuman Plan in his maiden speech in the Commons and had been Harold Macmillan's chief negotiator in 1961–2, took the realistic view, a view which was shared by Whitehall, that it would not be possible to secure from outside significant changes either in the CAP or the method of Community funding. Instead, he sought to get agreement on phasing, on a commitment to an 'equitable solution' of Britain's budgetary contributions once the transitional period was over, and on the creation of the European Regional Development Fund (from which it was hoped Britain would benefit). His approach was successful in achieving British entry. Its disadvantage was that it stored up trouble for the future. Even so, Edward Heath will be deservedly remembered as the man who took Britain into the European Community.

### 'Wading in Shit'

On 1 January 1973, Britain was welcomed into the European Community with high expectations. The original Six hoped that the British would bring with them not only their celebrated pragmatism and traditional respect for democratic values and institutions but also a new sense of purpose and commitment. Instead, they found us carping, unconstructive and, above all, ambivalent about our role in the Community.

The British resented becoming one of the paymasters of the Community, when in terms of per capita income Britain was now one of the poorest members. Nor could they bring themselves to accept a CAP which underwrote wasteful overproduction or a Community budget which allocated two-thirds of its spending to agriculture in which less than 10 per cent of the EC labour-force was employed. What was even more galling was the failure of British industry to take full advantage of access to a market of 250 million. Although trade with the EC expanded considerably, the United Kingdom consistently ran a trade deficit with the rest of the Community. To make matters worse, British entry coincided with the end of the period of European super growth, characteristic of the 1950s and 60s. Partly as a consequence of the two oil shocks of 1973 and 1979, the 1970s was a decade of low output, high inflation and rising unemployment. So the strains of adjustment were accentuated by economic stagnation throughout the EC.

The Labour Party's split over the EC made it even harder for Britain to adopt a constructive position. Following the February 1974 general election, the Heath administration was succeeded by a Labour government, led by Harold Wilson. As was described in Chapter 1, in 1962 Hugh Gaitskell had opposed EC entry on the terms negotiated by the Conservative government. However, in 1967 his successor as Labour leader, Harold Wilson, now prime minister, had made an application for membership which was blocked by de Gaulle (see Chapter 2). In opposition after 1970, Wilson faced strong party pressure to go into reverse and come out against the Common Market. Although the EC was never a straighforward left/right issue inside the Labour Party (see Chapter 7), the main support for the anti-market position came from the left, led by a radicalised Tony Benn. In 1968, Benn, then minister of technology, had said that 'the full benefits of an integrated European technology can only be achieved when Britain is a member of the EEC'.[14] In opposition, Benn switched posture, now arguing that acceptance of the Treaty of Rome would mean parliament ceding the right to make and execute laws to an unaccountable Brussels bureaucracy. He also convinced himself that EC membership would prevent industrial intervention by government. An astute populist campaigner, he advocated a referendum on the EC issue.

Wilson, by nature a conciliator and intent both on preserving his leadership and keeping his party together, gave ground. Following the completion of the negotiations, the Labour Party officially opposed British entry on terms achieved by Heath. However, Roy Jenkins, deputy leader, shadow chancellor, and Labour's leading common marketeer, refused to stand on his head. He and sixty-eight other Labour MPs (including Roy Hattersley and John Smith) defied a three line whip and voted for entry, while twenty Labour MPs abstained, thus ensuring a Commons majority of 112 for British membership.

Wilson also supported an amendment to the European Communities Bill which demanded a referendum before Britain could sign the treaty, at which point Roy Jenkins resigned as deputy leader. Subsequently, the Labour Party fought the February 1974 election on the policy of renegotiating the terms of entry and putting them to the people either through a referendum or a general election. Denis Healey, who succeeded Jenkins as shadow chancellor and became chancellor in the 1974 Labour government, has some sympathy with Wilson's predicament as leader of the opposition. He quotes Wilson as telling his shadow cabinet colleagues: 'I've been wading in shit for three months to allow others to indulge their conscience.'[15] However, Roy Jenkins has a good point when he comments that 'the handling of the European question by the leadership throughout the 1970s did more to cause the party's disasters of the 1980s than did any other issue'.[16]

The immediate consequence of Labour's somersault on the EC in opposition was that most of the two years following the February 1974 election was devoted not to developing a positive European position, but to renegotiating the terms of British membership. The renegotiations, conducted by the shrewd foreign secretary, James Callaghan, were, to a considerable extent, shaped by internal Labour Party considerations. The gains were, in the end, marginal. Wilson made great play about securing a better deal for the Commonwealth, boasting of his forty-four relations in New Zealand. The government secured a trade and aid package for the developing countries of the Commonwealth through the Lomé Convention, some improvement in the Commonwealth sugar agreements, and access for New Zealand butter beyond 1977. On the crucial question of the United Kingdom's budgetary contribution, a formula was devised whereby a member state would receive a rebate (limited to about £125 million in any one year) if it contributed more to the total budget than its appropriate percentage of its total gross domestic product. The establishment of the principle of a rebate was useful but the mechanism was inadequte and the actual sums involved were never likely to be enough.

A majority of the cabinet voted to accept the renegotiated terms which were also supported by a big majority in the Commons. However, a special Labour Party conference voted by 2 to 1 against acceptance.

The Labour government, was, therefore in the bizarre position of recommending to the country a deal which it was official Labour Party policy to oppose. However, in the subsequent referendum, the combination of the leading Labour cabinet ministers, the overwhelming majority of the Tory and Liberal parties and prominent figures in industry and the media was far too strong for the disparate opponents of British membership. The outcome was an overwhelming 2 to 1 endorsement for staying in the Community, though the result might have been different if the question had been whether or not to join. The verdict of the voters finally decided the issue of British membership. It did not, however, resolve the question of what kind of member Britain was to be.

James Callaghan, who succeeded Harold Wilson as prime minister in April 1976, was by inclination as much an 'Atlanticist' as Anthony Eden had been. However, his experience as foreign secretary had taught him that the European Community worked in a far more flexible way than he expected and could provide a solid foundation for British diplomacy. As prime minister, he sensibly developed close relations with the German chancellor, Helmut Schmidt, and the French president, Valéry Giscard d'Estaing. On occasions he was able to use these personal ties to build bridges between the United States and the European Community. Callaghan was acknowledged to have played a crucial part in putting together the package of measures which emerged from the Bonn economic summit of 1978.[17]

But if Callaghan understood that Britain's foreign policy had now to be based on the European Community, Britain continued to appear too negative in the debates over the internal development of the Community. The British dragged their feet over direct elections to the European Parliament and the government's handling of the British presidency of the Council of the Ministers in the first half of 1977 was considered by other member states to have been too partisan. In 1977, James Callaghan's letter to Ron Hayward, general secretary of the Labour Party, setting out the government's policy on the EC caused offence in other Community capitals. Part of the explanation was his scepticism, one which was widely shared across the political spectrum, towards further European integration. But an equally important reason was to placate EEC critics inside his own cabinet.

The most important EC development during Callaghan's premiership was the launch of the European Monetary System (EMS) in 1979. Characteristically, Britain declined to become a full member. The purpose of the EMS, which was inspired by a speech by the EC Commission president, Roy Jenkins, in October 1977, was to create a zone of monetary stability in Europe. Though it was enthusiastically backed by Schmidt and Giscard, Callaghan held aloof from the exchange rate mechanism (ERM). The reaction of the senior British Treasury adviser was revealing: 'But it is very bold, Prime Minister. It leaves the dollar on one side. I do not know what the Americans will say about it.'[18] In his memoirs, Callaghan himself emphasises that he was concerned about the possible deflationary consequences of being tied in at too high a rate, and about the reaction in the Labour Party.[19] Once again the British had refused to join a new EC institution at the outset and once again the leadership of the Community had been left firmly in French and German hands.

### English Nationalism Rides Again

At the 1979 election, Labour was decisively defeated by the Conservatives, led by Mrs Thatcher. As leader of the opposition, she had supported British membership of the European Community but her approach was very different from that of her predecessor, Edward Heath. The guiding principle of Mrs Thatcher's European policy was a British version of Gaullism, best illustrated by her celebrated September 1988 Bruges speech. Her vision of Europe, in so far as she had one, was a Europe of nation states: Mrs Thatcher asserted that 'willing and active cooperation between independent sovereign states is the best way to build a successful European Community'. She firmly rejected plans for further integration, as advocated by Jacques Delors.[20] She accepted that Britain was a European power but continuned to emphasise Britain's wider role and the special relationship with the United States.

Mrs Thatcher's style in Europe was uncompromisingly nationalistic. The first phase of her premiership was devoted to securing an effective and permanent rebate mechanism for Britain – getting 'her own money back' as she insensitively put it. A series of bad-tempered and inconclusive summits were preoccupied by the linked problems of the CAP, the EC budget and the British contribution. Finally, after Mrs Thatcher had characteristically overplayed her hand, an abatement formula was reached at Fontainebleau in 1984.

It might have been expected that, post-Fontainebleau, Mrs Thatcher, who by then was one of Europe's longest surviving leaders, would develop a more positive agenda. Indeed, her initiative on her plan to complete the internal market gave her an issue on which she could agree with Britain's partners. The Single European

Act, which was agreed at Luxemburg in December 1985, represented a compromise between the British commitment to the internal market and the acceptance by most other members of the extension of modified majority voting within the Council of Ministers. Again at the February 1988 Brussels European Council, Mrs Thatcher, after a year's divisive wrangling, did finally agree to a deal which combined tight controls on the CAP (which she supported), with an increase in Community income, a change in the method of Community funding and a doubling of the structural funds (all of which she opposed).

However, the Brussels agreement was a false dawn. In 1988 Mrs Thatcher publicly clashed with the man who had become her *bête noire*, Jacques Delors, the president of the Commission, on the future of the European Community. She bitterly opposed the Commission's proposal for a social dimension to accompany the internal market, while, both in her Bruges speech and her speech at the Conservative party conference, she attacked the idea of further integration which Delors argued would be the inevitable result of the creation of a single market. Ignoring the support given to these ideas by leading Christian Democrats, such as Helmut Kohl, the Belgian prime minister, Wilfried Martens, and the Dutch prime minister, Ruud Lubbers, she tried to portray the activities of Delors and the European Commission as a quasi-socialist conspiracy. For Mrs Thatcher, the brew of anti-socialism, anti-Europeanism and English nationalism was an irresistible but ultimately self-defeating mixture.

For the first time, Mrs Thatcher's negative posture on Europe met resistance not only from within her own party but also from the voters. In June 1989, the

Conservatives lost the European elections (see Chapter 7). The Labour Party, under Neil Kinnock's leadership, had abandoned the anti-EC position which the party had adopted in 1980. While the Tories concentrated on a negative attack on the EC Commission, Labour fought on a common manifesto with other European socialist parties and won forty-two seats to a Conservative total of thirty-one.

It was the issue of European monetary policy, however, which brought Mrs Thatcher's downfall. She had consistently opposed British membership of the exchange rate mechanism (ERM). She told Roy Jenkins that she was in favour of it in principle but 'nervous of being locked in at too low a rate of exchange, which will prevent my dealing with inflation' (symmetrically opposite to James Callaghan's fears).[21] But her opposition was as much nationalist and ideological as technical. She simply did not want decisions on exchange rate movement in the hands of the Bundesbank. Her refusal to join the ERM led to the resignation in October 1989 of the chancellor, Nigel Lawson, who had argued for British membership since 1985. A year later, against her inclinations, Mrs Thatcher was persuaded by John Major, Nigel Lawson's successor as chancellor, and by the foreign secretary, Douglas Hurd, to agree to Britain joining the ERM. But by 1990 the argument had moved on. The issue was now economic and monetary union (EMU).

In 1989, a committee primarily of central bankers, chaired by Jacques Delors, had proposed a three stage plan for EMU, culminating in a single currency. Mrs Thatcher was vehemently opposed to the principle of a single currency. Following the Rome summit of 27 and 28 October 1990 at which Britain had been totally isolated, Mrs Thatcher made a passionate defence of her position in the House of Commons. She told MPs that EMU was a threat to national identity and to parliamentary sovereignty and was the 'backdoor to a Federal Europe'. Her words may have pleased the anti-Europeans but they were too much for her deputy prime minister, Sir Geoffrey Howe, who resigned a few days later and then launched a fierce attack on her European policy.

Sir Geoffrey Howe's electrifying resignation speech in November 1990, which set in motion the train of events which led to the prime minister's resignation, should be seen not only as a damning indictment of Mrs Thatcher's European policy but also a devastating verdict on Britain's post-war relationship with the Continent.[22] He vehemently criticised the anti-European prejudices of Mrs Thatcher who saw the Continent as 'positively teeming with ill intentioned people' scheming to extinguish democracy, to undermine our national identity and to lead us through the back door to a federal Europe. He went on to say that the EC was 'not a zero sum game' and that participation in it ought to be considered not in the negative sense of surrendering national sovereignty but of pooling activities with other countries for the greater good. He also rejected Mrs Thatcher's attitude to economic and monetary union because it risked 'minimizing our influence and maximizing our chances of being once again shut out'. He concluded with a powerful warning, 'We have paid heavily in the past for the late starts and squandered opportunities in Europe. We dare not let that happen again.'

Three times since the war, over the Schuman Plan in 1950, over the Common Market in 1955–7, and over the European Monetary System in the late 1970s and 1980s, the British have missed crucial opportunities in Europe. When they have been eventually forced to join in, they complain that the rules have been set against them. It must not happen again. Commenting on Maastricht, Roy Hattersley, then deputy leader of the Opposition, summed up the British dilemma, using a 'bus' rather than a 'boat' metaphor: 'The cliché is that we missed the bus, but that is only part of the problem. The real tragedy is that we are destined to run along behind it and one day scramble on board even if it is then deviating from the route that we would have chosen.'[23]

**Left:** A characteristically rude Gillray cartoon from the Revolutionary Wars. John Bull, potent symbol of English nationalism, bombards the French 'bum-boats' in 1793.

L'Impudique Albion

**Left:** 'L'Impudique Albion.' Another 'posterior' cartoon, this time by the French cartoonist, Jean Veber. The face of the popular but slightly scandalous Edward VII is imprinted on the backside of a shameless Britannia.

**THE BRITISH CHARACTER**
TENDENCY TO KEEP OUT OF FOREIGN POLITICS

These *Punch* cartoons of the 1930s illustrate the British 'offshore' mentality.

**Above**: 'Tendency to keep out of foreign politics.' Notice the lofty but mildly irritated disinterest of the two British tourists. They clearly expect continentals to be unreliable and excitable.

**Above right**: 'Tendency to be embarrassed by foreign currencies.' Today the British are more familiar with foreign currencies, though they still have a strong attachment to sterling. However, a single European currency would get rid of all embarrassment.

**Below right**: 'Skill at foreign language.' The national 'hang-up' over learning languages remains a serious stumbling block to the British becoming enthusiastic Europeans.

**THE BRITISH CHARACTER**

TENDENCY TO BE EMBARRASSED BY FOREIGN CURRENCIES

**THE BRITISH CHARACTER.**

SKILL AT FOREIGN LANGUAGES.

*" VOILA, THIS IS WHAT YOU CALL 'HIT FOR SIX', NON ..?"*

**De Gaulle's revenge.** De Gaulle twice vetoed British entry to the EC. The crushing humiliation which De Gaulle inflicted on the British is indicated in these 1960s cartoons by the overpowering size of the French President compared to the puny figures of the two British Prime Ministers, Harold Macmillan and Harold Wilson. He is even beating us at cricket!

British isolation at the Maastricht Summit in December 1991 is splendidly captured in this *Economist* cover. While John Major adopts a 'pick and choose' *à la carte* approach, the other eleven sign up for European integration.

**Above:** When asked in a *Spectator* interview in July 1990 whether he preferred Kohl to Hitler, Nicholas Ridley, then Secretary of State for Industry, replied: 'I am not sure I wouldn't rather have the shelters and the chance to fight than simply being taken over by economics.' Ridley was forced to resign.

**Right:** This cartoon by Lurie which appeared in the *Frankfurter Allgemeine Zeitung* in the run up to Maastricht reflects the view about Britain's negative posture on Europe which is widely held in Germany.

# PART II

# Joining the Mainland

# – 5 –

# *European Destiny*

A good vantage point from which to view Britain's relationship with the mainland of Europe is the North American continent. When I am in the United States, I feel European. Despite the common language, the USA feels more foreign to me than do the countries of Continental Europe. The reason is that one misses the familiar European reference points – the old cities and towns, the medieval churches and cathedrals, the long-settled landscape. Most Britons in America discover they belong more to a European than an Atlantic or Anglo-Saxon civilisation.

Britain is part of Europe. Geographically, it is a group of islands off the mainland of Europe. Historically and culturally, it has always been closely tied to the Continent. Our destiny lies in the European Community.

## Shared Experience
From the earliest times, the British Isles have shared a common experience with the Continent. These include the Megalith phase; the Celtic period; the legacy of the Roman Empire; the pervasive influence of Christian Europe; the Renaissance; the European Enlightenment

121

of the late seventeenth and eighteenth centuries; the Industrial Revolution, of which Britain was the pioneer; and the imperialist expansion of which Britain was the leading exponent. A recent historian of Europe convincingly argues that 'there has long been a community of Europe – embryonic at first, but growing with time, despite centuries of war and conflict, blood and tears'.[1] Britain has always been part of that underlying European community.

The evidence of our common culture with the European mainland is all around us. Looking out, as I write, from the top of a south Lincolnshire hill, I can count six parish churches and one great cathedral. If I was on a Bavarian, Burgundian or Umbrian hill, I would almost certainly be able to spot a similar number of ecclesiastical buildings which, if somewhat different in style, would recognisably belong to the same Christian civilisation. Going north, if you cross the Tyne at Newcastle, you can see a magnificent Plantagenet castle, built by Henry II (1154–89). There are similar castles not only throughout the British Isles but also in Normandy, Brittany, the Loire, and further south in the Limousin, Angoulême and Périgord, either built or restored by Henry whose energy, according to the medieval chronicler, Walter Map, disturbed 'almost half Christendom'. This reminds us that, in the twelfth century, England belonged to a powerful Angevin empire which stretched across the Channel far to the south-west of France.

On my bookshelves, I have a copy of John Locke's second *Treatise of Civil Government* (published in 1690) which put forward the notion of limited government and championed the concept of civil liberties. Next to it is his *Essay on Human Understanding* (also published in 1690) in which he set out what he believed

122

to be the laws controlling the formation of human ideas. Locke was very much a European who spent five years on the Continent in exile in the Netherlands before returning to England with William of Orange to become the political and moral philosopher of the 'Glorious Revolution'. His ideas influenced Montesquieu and Voltaire not only in their powerful critiques of French eighteenth-century despotism but also in their view of the world.

In the age of the Enlightenment, European ideas, in their turn, impressed the British. The upper classes went to the Continent to acquire a smattering of history, politics and philosophy – sometimes directly from the 'star' teachers. Adam Smith, for example, counted himself as fortunate to be allowed to sit at Voltaire's feet.[2] Edward Gibbon visited Voltaire at Ferney, his country house: 'Shew me in history or fable, a famous poet of seventy who has acted in his own plays, and has closed the scene with a supper and a ball for a hundred people.'[3] Voltaire described this cultural interchange as a kind of 'Europe of the mind':

> The peoples of Europe share humane principles which are not found in other parts of the world. ... Christian Europeans are as the ancient Greeks used to be: they may go to war with each other, but despite these conflicts they do observe the proprieties ... that a Frenchman and Englishman and a German, when they meet, often seem as if they were born in the same town.[4]

It helped that everybody in this class spoke French. The dramatic changes of the nineteenth century – the Industrial Revolution, the spread of capitalism and the explo-

123

sive expansion of trade – forged new links between Britain and the rest of the world, including mainland Europe. The great Exhibition of 1851 in London, to which six million British and foreign visitors came, was a giant international display of industrial progress. It was followed by exhibitions in Paris and Vienna. The 'Age of Capital' was unashamedly internationalist.[5]

But industrialisation had its dark side. It was the inhumane treatment and appalling conditions not only in Britain but across the Continent which led workers to combine together in trade unions and form socialist parties. Like the capitalists, these labour movements were also internationalist, fervently putting their proletarian solidarity before their national loyalty. The founder of my union, the General, Municipal and Boilermakers' Union, was Will Thorne, who was taught to read and write by Eleanor Marx, Karl Marx's daughter. At the turn of the century, he was an eager participant at a number of meetings of the Second International at which French, German and other European socialists denounced the evils of nationalism and fulminated against the horrors of war. Yet when war broke out in 1914, the majority of socialist and trade union leaders, including Thorne, supported the war effort.

If the age of nationalism, industrial competition, and imperialism in the late nineteenth and early twentieth centuries sharply divided nations, war was a catastrophic experience which most of Europe shared. Just inside my grandfather's front door was a brass shell case, used as a doorstop. It was a memento brought back from the 1914–18 war. Like millions of Britons, he had crossed the Channel to fight for his country in Flanders and Northern France. Three decades later, his son was a soldier in the great allied army which liberated France and defeated Hitler.

Involvement in two European wars should have been enough to convince the British that their fate was tied to the Continent. Yet, because they were on the winning side, they thought they could revert to their old isolationist ways. Britain rejected proposals for European union put forward by mainland countries which, in defeat, had lost confidence in the traditional nation states as 'the self sufficient framework of political life'.[6] But the British attempt to stand aloof from Continental developments was never likely to be viable in the second half of the twentieth century. It is certainly not a credible policy today. Commenting on options for British foreign policy in the 1990s, two Chatham House authors note that 'one of the most striking aspects of Britain's current position is the extent to which it has become a West European state, first and foremost'.[7]

The British economy has become closely linked to a West European economic system, in which Germany is predominant. The shift in the pattern of British trade is striking. In 1961, when Britain first applied to join the Common Market, only a third of its trade was with EC and EFTA countries. Today, as much as two-thirds of British trade is with Western Europe, while Germany has become Britain's single most important trading partner. The decision to join the Exchange Rate Mechanism (ERM) in October 1990 was an admission that Britain was already part of a D Mark zone. With membership of the ERM, the completion of the single market by the end of 1992, and the prospect of economic and monetary union by the end of the 1990s the British economy will become even more deeply enmeshed with the other economies of Western Europe.

In January 1948, faced by the growing threat from the Soviet Union, Ernest Bevin told the House of Commons: 'Britain cannot stand outside Europe and regard her problems as quite separate from those of her European neighbours.'[8] Strategically, Britain has been committed to Western European security since the beginning of the cold war. The Treaties of Dunkirk and Brussels and, more decisively, the setting up of the North Atlantic Treaty Organisation in 1949 involved the British in the defence of Europe. Following the collapse of the proposal for a European Defence Community in 1953, the British government pledged itself in the 1954 Western European Union treaty to maintain four divisions and a tactical airforce on West German soil. Since then, the 55,000 British troops on NATO's central front in West Germany have represented an important contribution to European security.

Although, with the end of the cold war, there is an overwhelming case for major cuts in the British defence contribution (as envisaged in the 1991 Defence White Paper), it will remain a vital British interest to co-operate with other nations to ensure Europe's security. Even after the collapse of Soviet power in Eastern Europe, the demise of the Warsaw Pact, and the disintegration of the Soviet Union, British forces will be required on the Continent to help deal with conflicts that could arise either within or outside Europe.

Our foreign policy is becoming increasingly European. Ever since it first joined the European Community, Britain has co-ordinated its foreign policy with its community partners through the European Political Co-operation framework. The co-ordination has provided a reinforcement which successive British foreign secretaries have learnt to appreciate. Sir Geoffrey Howe once remarked that he saw more of his opposite numbers from France, Germany and other leading European countries than he saw of some of his colleagues in the British Cabinet.[9] Douglas Hurd told the House of Commons in June 1991 that he understood more clearly day by day the advantages of working together in foreign policy. He added: 'Divided, each of us individually would make a weaker impact than when we act together.'[10]

For Britain, there really is no alternative to European integration. It is not just that the so-called options put forward at one time or another by the anti-Europeans – the Commonwealth, EFTA, a North Atlantic Free Trade Area, a union of English-speaking peoples, a fortress Britain – have all proved to be chimeras. It is not merely that we have been a member of the EC and all that has involved since 1973. The crucial point is that Britain is a medium-sized, post-imperial power, linked to the Continent not only be geography, history and culture but also by economics, politics and security.

### The Illusion of Sovereignty

Some critics argue that it would be possible for Britain to become a kind of 'country member' of the EC by remaining part of the customs union but opting out of any further economic and monetary or political obligation. The Conservative MP, Teddy Taylor, suggested a 'two-speed' Europe with Britain in the 'slow lane', while former Cabinet minister, Nicholas Ridley, predicted that 'outside EMU, but in the single market . . . we could become the financial centre of the world, the Hong Kong of mainland Europe'.[11]

It is, of course, hardly novel for the British either to attempt to dilute Continental proposals or to seek a special position for Britain. Jean Monnet's comment about British tactics is apposite here: 'Their national character inclines them to see a special position which will save them from having to change.'[12] The flaw, however, with such proposals is that, in practice, our economy would continue to be heavily influenced by decisions in EC countries, especially Germany, without us being able to participate in the institutional arrangements from which these decisions largely flowed.

At the heart of the controversy over Britain's role in Europe is, as it has always been, the issue of sovereignty. Here advocates of EC membership have sometimes been less than candid. The 1971 White Paper arguing for entry stated there was 'no question of any erosion of essential national sovereignty'. The main reason for joining, according to supporters, was that a larger market would benefit Britain economically. The sovereignty question was ducked, except by outright opponents like Enoch Powell and Tony Benn. Powell told the 1971 Conservative Party conference that he did not become 'a member of our sovereign Parliament in order to consent to that sovereignty being abated or transferred'.[13] In the 1975 referendum, Benn argued that 'continued membership of the Community . . . means the end of Britain as a completely self-governing nation and of our democractically elected Parliament as the supreme law-making body of the United Kingdom.'[14]

The truth is that joining the European Community *did* involve a loss of formal sovereignty in trade and other areas, above all agriculture. As the EC has progressed since 1973, there has been a further erosion of national sovereignty. As European integration speeds up in the 1990s, especially if economic and monetary union is achieved, some of the crucial powers of a nation state will be transferred to the European Community. But the absolutist view of national sovereignty put forward by Enoch Powell and Tony Benn is excessively abstract. As was argued in Chapter 1, it is derived from an outdated theory of parliamentary sovereignty which, in its exceptionalist claims, shows a disregard for individual and community rights. It is also unrealistic because it ignores the fact that, in or out of the EC, the freedom to act of a medium-sized state is seriously circumscribed.

For over forty years (and especially since the 1961 Nassau agreement over Polaris) Britain has effectively depended on the United States for its defence. Over the last twenty years, the development of capital and other financial markets has drastically reduced our autonomy in the management of our economic affairs. Even if Britain had remained outside the European Community, we would have been greatly affected by decisions on trade and on economic and monetary matters taken by EC members, especially Germany. There are even limitations on American power. Former US secretary of state, George Shultz, who ought to know, sums up the position as follows:

> Borders are becoming porous, almost irrelevant, in more and more areas of sovereign importance: money, ideas, information, missiles. So, the concept of absolute sovereignty is long gone. The model of divided sovereignty – part of the fabric of our own country since its birth – has become applicable on the international scene at large.[15]

Sir Geoffrey Howe, with his pragmatic lawyer's mind, has pointed out that sovereignty 'is not virginity, which you either have or you don't . . . rather it is . . . a never-ending series of transactions between nation states, handing over some things and taking back others'.[16] He argues for a modern approach to sovereignty, defined as a nation's practical capacity to maximise its influence in the world. Thus Britain joined the European Community to enhance its position, trading its formal sovereignty for a share in co-operative arrangements which would give it a greater say.

Belonging to the EC provides Britain with an opportunity to participate in decisions which vitally affect us, assisting us to achieve, in co-operation with our partners, what Winston Churchill called 'that larger sovereignty' and the French Socialist spokesman on Europe, Gérard Fuchs, has described as 'collective mastery of our destiny'.[17] Thus, in giving up a largely illusory sovereignty, we obtain real influence.

## Deepening and Widening

In the 1990s, the European Community, by deepening and widening, will dramatically increase both its internal cohesion and the range of its authority. At the same time, its power in the world will grow accordingly.

The momentum behind greater European integration is gathering speed. By the end of 1992, a wide range of decisions bringing EC members closer together will have been taken. These include the Single European Act and the completion of the internal market, the drive towards economic and monetary union, the adoption of the Social Charter, new common policies, the strengthening of Community institutions, and the tackling of the 'democratic deficit'. This burst of creativity, which comes after the stagnation of the late 1970s and early 1980s, has been so spectacular that one commentator has predicted that 'the years of 1985–93 will have replaced 1958–65 as the longest continuous period of institutional advance' in the history of European integration.[18]

At the same time, almost all the countries on its borders now wish to join the EC. During 1992, three of the prosperous EFTA countries, Sweden, Finland and Austria, applied for membership, and the rest are likely to follow suit. Three Mediterranean countries, Turkey, Cyprus and Malta, have also applied for membership. Most crucial of all, the former communist states of Eastern Europe, especially Hungary, Czechoslovakia and Poland, hope for eventual membership. The EC Commission's president, Jacques Delors, has predicted that, by the end of the decade, the EC's present membership of twelve could have expanded to at least twenty-four.[19]

The strengthening of the EC's authority in these ways will add significantly to its external influence. Already, the EC is the world's largest trading bloc, accounting for over 40 per cent of global trade. As such, it speaks on behalf of its members in the key GATT negotiations with the United States and Japan. If, as a consequence of economic and monetary union, the écu develops as a major international currency, it will increasingly represent them in other fora as well. In foreign and security policy, EC members will more and more speak with a common voice. By the year 2000, the EC will have assumed some of the attributes of a European superpower.

Some British anti-integrationists, however, believe

that there is a conflict between widening and deepening which is not only unbridgeable but will end in disaster for all Europeans. One distinguished columnist has even drawn a distinction between the good Europeans, 'who want to build a European Community of independent nations, as broad as possible in terms of its membership', and the bad Europeans, 'who want to turn the 12 . . . into a self protective federal club'.[20]

In my view, the sceptics are wrong. It will be essential for the EC both to deepen and widen. A European Community worthy of the name must include as many European states as possible. It must also build an economic and political framework strong enough to safeguard the security and prosperity of these states.

As candidates for membership, the EFTA countries present few problems. They have already agreed to a common market with the EC; all of them are Western democracies; and all of them have standards of living which are comparable with and, in some cases, superior to those of existing EC members. Their past objections to membership arose from fears either of compromising their neutral or special status (as with Austria, Sweden, Switzerland and Finland) or of losing sovereignty (as with Norway). The end of the cold war as well as the need to be a part of the European internal market and to participate in the EC's political framework has helped to change their minds. Although the existing members of the EC had tried to defer any decision about additional members until after 1992, at Maastricht they agreed to proceed with enlargement. The real argument is about the former communist states of Eastern Europe. All Western Europeans want to offer help and encouragement to these new democracies. Already the EC has given aid to a number of these countries and has signed association agreements with Poland, Hungary and Czechoslovakia leading to free trade. The prospect of membership is a potent motivating force in Eastern Europe. At the June 1990 elections in Czechoslovakia, for example, the main campaigning slogan of the electorally successful Civic Forum was 'with us to Europe'. Yet the problems of adapting the command economies of countries like Poland, Czechoslovakia and Hungary to the fierce competition of the EC single market are formidable.

The critics argue that the difficulties of adapting to a common market would be compounded by the adoption of a single European currency. Mrs Thatcher warned the Commons in June 1991 that there was no way 'in which the economies of the former Communist states of Eastern Europe could withstand the pressure placed on their fragile industries by a single currency – witness what has happened to Eastern Germany'.[21] But the East German monetary union is a poor analogy. In July 1990 Chancellor Kohl's government took the decision, under pressure from the East Germans and against the advice of the Bundesbank, to create a single all-Germany currency at the artifically inflated rate of 1 DM for 1 Ostmark, instead of 1 DM for 5 or 6 Ostmarks. Kohl's objective was political – to halt the flood of East German refugees and to help win the forthcoming all-German Federal elections. He succeeded in the latter but not in the former. Nobody, least of all President Havel of Czechoslovakia, President Walesa of Poland or Prime Minister Antall of Hungary, is advocating such a hasty move for Eastern Europe.

What is actually being proposed for and accepted by the East Europeans is a substantial period of preparation and adaptation before joining the EC. Member-

133

ship would also be accompanied by lengthy transitional arrangements (as in the case of Spain and Portugal). When these countries finally decide to join the single European currency, it will be at a far more realistic rate than with German monetary union. So further economic integration by existing EC members will not prevent the former communist countries from joining the Community by the end of the century or soon after.

Enlargement, however, is likely to require far-reaching institutional changes. For example, it would no longer be possible to treat all Community languages as official because full membership for all six members of EFTA would produce a total of thirteen official languages. Nor would it be possible for the Council of Ministers to conduct its business by giving, say, eighteen ministers an equal say at every stage, as eighteen introductory statements would occupy around three hours. It would also make the extension of majority voting inevitable, otherwise community business would be in danger of being brought to a standstill. Other, far more reaching changes could well be needed.

Jacques Delors argues that a European Community of as many as twenty-four members will require a 'new political and institutional' framework.[22] It will certainly not be possible to tackle the problems of the twenty-first century by returning to the values and structures of the nineteenth century.

Closer union is needed to provide solutions where nation states, acting by themselves, patently fail – for example, in securing economic and monetary stability, in achieving acceptable environmental standards, and in developing effective foreign and security policies. Closer union will give its members greater clout in the world. It will enable them to give more effective aid to other countries, including the states of Eastern Europe. Above all, only a strong European union will be able to cope with the disastrous legacy that the collapse of the Soviet empire has bequeathed to its successors. In short, deepening is an essential prerequisite of widening.

## The Case for EMU

A key element in deepening is the accord on European Economic and Monetary Union (EMU). In December 1991, the European Council agreed on a staged programme to set up a European Central Bank and establish a single currency by the end of the decade, though with an opt-out clause designed for Britain.

The former Conservative chancellor, Nigel Lawson, has cautioned against the 'misguided enterprise' of a single currency because it could lead to the 'ugliest manifestation of nationalism', while Mrs Thatcher's close ally, Norman Tebbit, has predicted the rise of fascist movements if countries see their 'destiny governed by people overseas'.[23] Cassandras point to the Italian election and to setbacks to the French and German governments in the Spring of 1992 as evidence of popular rejection.

But EMU is not some hare-brained scheme, dreamed up by power-crazed Europeans. It is a set of practical proposals with firm roots in the increasing integration of the European economies, a process which is being strengthened by the completion of the single market, especially in its impact on financial services. Helmut Schmidt once asked, 'Who ever heard of a single market with eleven currencies?'[24] It is based on the undoubted success of the ERM in providing greater monetary coordination and stability during the 1980s. Its backing comes not only from European politicians but also, as the strong support from the CBI demonstrates, from hard-headed businessmen who have weighed up the benefits to be derived from a single currency.

The advantages for business of monetary union are that it ends transaction costs, eliminates exchange-rate instability and provides a stable environment for economic growth. The EC Commission has estimated the saving in the transaction costs involved in changing money from one currency to another of more than 15 billion écus each year. More important for industry, however, is the prospect of being able to plan trade and investment without having to worry about currency fluctuations. No wonder that British firms, which have had to suffer so much from the dramatic hikes and falls in the value of the pound over the last decade, are such strong supporters.

As far as the economic policy makers are concerned, a monetary union would end the rate of the exchange rate as a means of adjustment. But in a world of global markets in which currency flows are related more to potential movements in interest rates rather than to economic performance, devaluation has lost most of its attraction. There is certainly still a case for a measure of autonomy as regards fiscal policy as a way of compensating for economic shocks, as well as a strong regional policy to assist convergence. But the loss of exchange rate flexibility will not be a serious disadvantage for EC members. The firm monetary framework provided by EMU is a more than adequate compensation.

In more general terms, a single currency across the Community would give the Europeans increased bargaining power *vis à vis* the dollar and the yen. The EC would acquire greater influence on American and Japanese policy makers and more authority in international monetary policy.

France, Italy and the Benelux countries also support EMU because it would give them a voice in the management of European monetary policy. Although their economies have benefited from ERM, they rightly believe that the ERM has been run by the German Bundesbank. Even Britain, which has recently joined the ERM, has effectively been part of the DM zone throughout much of the 1980s. The choice, as French European Commissioner, Christiane Scrivener, has pointed out, is between a dominant or a single currency. A seat on the European Central Bank, as well as an element of accountability through the Economic and Finance Committee of the Council of Ministers, would give the other EC members, including Britain, a say in monetary policy.

Behind this desire for a greater say in European monetary matters lies a more general concern, especially in France, about the Federal Republic's greater strength and influence following unification. As in 1950 over the Schuman Plan, so forty years later President Mitterrand sought to contain German power within a common European framework, to create, as Thomas Mann put it, 'a European Germany, not a German Europe'.[25] In Germany itself the Bundesbank is cautious about EMU, partly because it fears that other countries may undermine Germany's achievements on the inflationary front. But Chancellor Kohl and Foreign Minister Genscher support EMU mainly on political grounds, because they hope it will assuage other countries' doubts about Germany.

The Major government's motive in seeking and

obtaining the right to 'opt out' of the third stage of EMU was to a considerable extent narrowly party-political. John Major sought to prevent a split in the Conservative Party by postponing a decision on a single currency. There is a more respectable argument for delay which turns on the need to promote convergence between the British *and* the German and French econ-omies. There is undoubtedly an underlying gap in inflation, growth, and above all, productivity, which must be closed. However, although a European single currency is not likely to be established much before the end of the century, the Major government ought to commit itself to the principle now. Improving the performance of the British economy will certainly take time but it is far more likely to be achieved if it is placed firmly in a European framework.

One reason why Britain has attracted considerable investment in recent years, especially from the US and Japan, is that it has been a member of the EC. The 'opt out' clause is bound to raise doubts about Britain's future. If British politicians hesitate too long, inward investment will switch to the members of the EMU 'fast track', particularly to France and Germany, while London would cease to be Europe's leading financial centre. If, on the other hand, Britain committed itself to the principle of a single currency and was an integral part of the move towards economic and monetary union, Britain would not only continue to attract invest-ment but also gain a stable economic and monetary framework within which to adapt its economy. In other words, accepting the prospect of a single currency would itself help promote the process of convergence.

Over the last forty years, Britain has missed a number of crucial opportunities in Europe. It is vital for the country's future that the British do not make the same mistake over EMU.

## 'Ever Closer Union'

British opponents of European integration believe that the agreements on economic and monetary union and political union reached in December 1991 have set the EC firmly on the road to federalism. Certainly, many of the founding fathers of the EC, including Paul-Henri Spaak, Walter Hallstein, Jean Monnet, Robert Marjolin and Sicco Mansholt, were federalists who hoped that one day the EC would become a federal state. Earlier drafts of the treaty on political union contained an introduction which proclaimed the EC's objective as being 'a union with a federal goal', though, at the British government's request, it was removed from the final text agreed at Maastricht.

What is meant by federalism? In some British political circles, particularly in the Conservative Party, it is a dirty word, conjuring up the image of a centralising European super state which inexorably steals away our national sovereignty. But on the Continent it is about the limitation and diffusion of power. This conflict of views reflects differences in political experience. As we have seen in Chapter 1, Britain is a unitary state, with parliament theoretically sovereign over all aspects of British life. In contrast, Germany and Belgium are federal states, while in Italy, Spain and even France power is far more decentralised than in Britain.

Continental Europeans points out that, in a federal state, central government is usually responsible for external relations and defence but its control over internal matters is tightly circumscribed. Whether or not the central government is relatively powerful, as in Germany, or relatively weak, as in Switzerland, the second-tier authorities have irreducible constitutional rights. They cannot be overridden or even abolished, as the Greater London Council was by Mrs Thatcher's administration. In addition, both central and regional governments are accountable to elected parliaments. So when Continentals talk of a federal Europe, they envisage a democratically accountable and legally defined system in which power is shared between the European institutions and the member states. They also emphasize the importance of 'subsidiarity' – a useful if somewhat arcane concept. According to the principle of 'subsidiarity', included in the political treaty, the EC should perform only those functions which it can carry out more effectively than member states acting separately. In other words, the EC's powers should be limited to those areas in which it does the job better than national governments. Subsidiarity is also about the role of public authority more generally.

One argument needs to be refuted. Anti-Europeans who point to the collapse of the Soviet Union as a warning against European union only demonstrate their lack of understanding. The move towards European union is not a shotgun marriage but an association of free peoples. Individual ministers in the Council of Ministers remain accountable to national parliaments, while, following the Maastricht agreement, the directly elected European Parliament is gradually gaining greater influence at EC level. Indeed, one would take critics more seriously if they were advocating more power to the European Parliament to control the unelected European Commission.

It is clear, however, that, even after the two treaties

have been implemented, the EC will still be some way from being a federal state. It will have strong federal aspects. Over trade, it already has the powers of a federation.[26] Externally, it controls the common tariff and common commercial policy. Internally, it polices the single market and competition policy. The free movement of capital, the integration of financial services, the discipline of ERM, and the impetus behind the EMU programme will give the EC overall monetary control. It has significant powers over environmental, labour-market and regional policies, which are strengthened in the new treaty.

The big gap is the EC's lack of overriding competence in foreign and defence policy. As was described above, the European Political Co-operation framework has been extensively and often effectively used to co-ordinate the foreign policies of member states, though on some major issues, especially over the Gulf crisis and the disintegration of Yugoslovia, the divergent attitudes and interests of member states has been only too apparent.

With respect to defence, there is no common European policy. Eleven out of the twelve member states belong to NATO, while nine belong to the WEU, whose role so far has been more deliberative than operative. But, as Jacques Delors pointed out in a speech to the Institute of Strategic Studies in March 1991, when, as in the Gulf War, force has to be used, the EC is powerless to act. It is this weakness on foreign policy and defence which, according to Professor Kennedy, has hampered the development of a more powerful and influential EC. He points out that the EC 'has the size, the wealth and productive capacity of a Great Power ... yet Europe's power and effectiveness in the world is much less than the crude total of its economic and military strength would suggest – simply because of disunity'.[27]

The political union treaty establishes the possibility, where the European Council agrees, of qualified majority voting in foreign policy. But foreign policy remains firmly under the control of the European Council, the intergovernmental power house of the EC. Although the prospect of a common European defence policy is not ruled out, defence matters are referred to the Western European Union: its members have agreed that it should act as a bridge between the European Community and NATO. Thus, though intergovernmental co-operation may have been strengthened in these crucial areas, the initiative on foreign policy and defence still remains firmly with national governments.

In the 1990s, the EC is still *sui generis*, partly federal, partly confederal. But it is undoubtedly gathering more power and influence. The British should recognise that, whatever precise constitutional form it takes, the EC is becoming an 'ever closer union', a union of which Britain must be an integral part. Britain's future lies in Europe.

# – 6 –

# *Citizens of Europe*

When in 1950, at the time of the Schuman Plan, Jean Monnet predicted that the British would 'adjust to the facts' as they saw that European integration had succeeded, he cannot have imagined that it would take so long.[1] However, by the beginning of the 1990s, the British people had come to accept the case for greater European unity. Equally important, powerful underlying forces were gradually binding Britain closer to the mainland.

## Changing our Minds

As was described in the first part of the book, the British have been extremely reluctant Europeans. Even when an overwhelming 67 per cent voted 'yes' in the 1975 referendum, this was more a vote against the uncertainties of coming out than positive backing for the EC. Indeed, for most of the first sixteen years of membership, only a minority, and on occasions below a quarter of the electorate, actually supported the EC.[2]

But at the end of the 1980s, a crucial shift took place in British public opinion. Since 1989, there has not only been majority support for EC membership but also

143

increased backing for many aspects of European integration. If the British still remain sceptical when asked in general terms about giving up sovereignty, overwhelming majorities back the right to work in any EC country, mutual recognition across the EC of qualifications and diplomas, the Social Charter and common policies for the environment.[3] It looks very much as if a majority of the British people have finally decided that the European Community is a good thing.

Why have the British changed their minds? They are a cautious people and it has taken them a long time to get used to being part of the EC. Now at last they are becoming accustomed to the idea. Another explanation is that the older generation, which came through the last war and which because of that experience tended to be the most anti-European, is gradually dying out. At the same time, a new generation is growing up which cannot remember what it was like to be outside the EC.

A further, perhaps more profound reason, is that the British are losing confidence in purely national solutions to problems. The polls show clearly that, in contrast to forty years ago, they now think that other European nations are better than them in running their economies, in managing their education, vocational training and transport systems and keeping their countries clean and tidy. The British are also increasingly inclined to opt for European policies when they believe them to be more effective. Above all, the British do not want to be excluded from future European developments. Even if they do not themselves benefit immediately from European integration, they want their children to be in a position to do so.[4]

The British are beginning to look to the European Community to compensate for national deficiencies. In so doing, they are following the example of other nations. Most Europeans support the unity of Europe not just because it is a fine ideal but because they believe it brings practical benefits to their countries. The Germans are enthusiastic Europeans because the EC legitimises German power and offers them an insurance policy against repeating past mistakes. The French like the European Community because it enables them to play a leading role in Europe and subsidises their agriculture. The Italians look to Europe to give them a direction and purpose which is not provided by their national governments. For the Spanish, the EC underwrites the modernisation and democratisation of their country. EC membership gives the smaller nations, like the Dutch and the Belgians, an opportunity to influence the decisions of the bigger powers. For them, the Community has been 'a fine ride in the forest of politics where they can at last command a view of their own futures'.[5] Now the British too are finding out that the EC can give them a view of their own future.

### The Impact of 1992

At the same time as the British are discovering the advantages of the EC, underlying economic, social and cultural factors are making them more European.

The most obvious influence is economic. The 1987 Single European Act committed the British government to the completion by 31 December 1992 of a single European market 'without internal frontiers in which the free movement of goods, persons, services and capital is ensured'. The impact on the British of a European home market will be considerable. The customs union created by the Treaty of Rome and which

145

Britain joined in 1973 was successful in eliminating tariff barriers between member states. As we have seen, its effect was to attach the British economy more closely to the other major economies of Western Europe. British firms became increasingly reliant on European markets, while British shoppers bought German, French, Italian and Benelux goods in ever increasing numbers.

But the results of the customs union fell well short of the common market which had been envisaged by the EC's creators. A plethora of obstacles prevented the genuinely free movement of goods, services, capital and persons across the Community. These included *physical* barriers such as border controls and customs red tape; *technical* barriers associated with divergent national product standards and technical regulations; and *fiscal* barriers in the form of differing rates of VAT and excise duties. In addition, national governments usually confined public procurement to domestic manufacturers and suppliers, while financial and other service markets were fragmented by regulation and restrictive practice. According to the Cecchini Report, published by the EC Commission in 1988, the cost of all these barriers is more than £140 billion. If they are successfully removed, then costs and prices would come down in a 'self-sustaining virtuous circle'. Consumer prices would be reduced by an average of 6.1 per cent and 4.5 per cent would be added to the Community's gross domestic product. Employment would be boosted by 1.8 million. In the medium term, room would also be created for governments to take action on unemployment, which would increase growth and jobs. Cecchini concluded that creating a genuine single market of 370 million would 'put Europe on an upward trajectory of economic growth lasting into the next century'.

There is not a simple, straightforward answer to the question, 'What's in it for Britain?' With respect to industry, some companies, for example those in car-manufacturing, footwear and clothing, are already operating on a European-wide basis. But, according to one survey, British firms in the high tech areas, in which there have often been substantial barriers to trade, should be well placed to benefit from the single market.[6] Britain has a comparative advantage in financial services, especially insurance and banking. In this field we should be able to withstand Continental competition and extend operations on the mainland. Our retailing industry is also probably the most efficient in the EC. However, much will depend on the response of British companies. The most successful will be those which are prepared to organise and market on a European scale. International companies like ICI and Unilever will have few problems. It is much more difficult for small- and medium-sized firms. Here the experience of Derwent Valley Foods, a successful North-East company employing about three hundred workers, is instructive. Although selling throughout Europe, Derwent Valley Foods have found it essential to study national tastes and tailor their products accordingly; in France, the cheese taste has to be like Roquefort; in Holland, less salt is used. In other words, though the objective is to sell throughout Europe, the national preference of consumers will have to be taken into account if firms are to succeed.

What can be said with certainty is that the British economy will become ever more closely linked to the other West European economies, a process which will be intensified by economic and monetary union. Businessmen and women, many of whom are already beginning to 'think European', will no longer have any alternative if they are to keep their jobs.

Speaking European languages will become even more essential than before. As Sir Peter Parker, a leading industrialist, bluntly puts it: 'Talking English louder is not enough'. Prince Charles, in a notable speech on the importance of languages on 23 August 1990, told the story of the exasperated French businessman who, after repeated attempts to get through on the telephone to his trading partner in Britain, sent the following telex in French: 'When we telephone, your operator does not understand French and simply cuts us off. You ought to explain to her that though English is certainly a marvellous language, it is not yet universal. If you wish to sell abroad, you will have, like other nations, to make an effort.' A 1988 survey of over 1100 British companies revealed that nearly half believed that they could improve their trade performance if more of their staff spoke European languages.[7] In the 1990s, it will be essential for the young men or women climbing the promotion ladder to become fluent in at least German and French.

So much for business. What about labour? Trade unionists who may have been hostile to the EC in the past now strongly support the 1992 programmes, though they rightly want it to include the protection of employee rights. Ron Todd, then general secretary of the Transport and General Workers' Union, told the TUC in 1988: 'The only card game in town at the moment is in a town called Brussels . . . we've got to learn the rules, and pretty fast'. The TUC is promoting links with Continental unions, while individual unions are educating their members about the implications of 1992.

Consumers, who have become accustomed to a cornucopia of Continental goods in supermarkets, will now get an even wider range of goods which should be cheaper in real terms than ever before. As a consequence of economic and monetary union, they may also be paying in écus, thus facilitating comparison with prices in other countries. The British may not yet feel European but increasingly their consumption patterns and style of living will be Continental. They will become like the English Lord Faulconbridge in *The Merchant of Venice* of whom Portia says, 'I think he bought his doublet in Italy, his round hose in France, his bonnet in Germany, and his behaviour everywhere.'

**Europe without Frontiers**
Getting rid of frontier controls within the Community is, as was described above, a key element in the economic part of the 1992 programme. Frontier controls and red tape were identified by business executives as the single greatest obstacle to the expansion of intra-Community trade. The Cecchini Report estimated that up to 25 per cent of company profits were eaten away by costs and delays at frontiers and that the situation was even worse for smaller companies.

But, as Jacques Delors has remarked 'It is hard to fall in love with a single market.'[8] Fortunately 1992 is not just about economics. It is also about free movement of peoples. In the days before mass air travel, the great British foreign secretary, Ernest Bevin, said that the aim of his foreign policy was 'to go down to Victoria Station, get a railway ticket, and go where the Hell I liked without a passport or anything else'.[9] The proposal to abolish frontier controls within the EC would make Bevin's splendid traveller's dream a reality.

Not surprisingly, abolition of frontiers receives enthusiastic popular support from Europeans, including the British. The enormous expansion of tourism over the last thirty years has made national borders seem pointless. The British are, after the Germans, Europe's keenest tourists.[10] They go in their millions to France and the Iberian peninsula. Greece, Italy and Germany are also favourite British destinations. Sadly the British government has been dragging its feet over abolition of frontier controls. While the so-called Schengen Group has already agreed to abolish most of the controls between France, Germany and the Benelux countries, and later Spain, Italy and Portugal, the British government has argued that frontier checks in Britain are necessary as a weapon in the fight against terrorism illegal immigration and drugs. However, in the view of one expert, the British island border controls 'provide a false sense of security and run the risk of becoming obstacles to the fight against transnational crime'.[11] In any case, pressure from travellers and traders is almost certain to persuade Britain to modify its position. In the 1990s there will be simply no stopping the phenomenal cross-border summer migration movement in which the British already play such a prominent part.

As important as the abolition of frontier controls in bringing Britain closer to the Continent will be the opening of the Channel Tunnel in 1993. Lord Randolph Churchill told the House of Commons in 1889: 'The reputation of England has hitherto depended on her being, as it were *virgo intacta*.' But the opening of the tunnel means that Britain's hesitant marriage to the European Community in January 1973 will have been 'physically consummated'.[12] The British government has been far slower than the French government in developing the high-speed rail links between the Channel and inland cities. But eventually, being able to get on a train not only in London but in Birmingham, Manchester, Newcastle and Edinburgh and stay on it to Paris and beyond is bound to have a profound psychological impact. It will literally be the end of our island story.

A vital aspect of the unimpeded movement of people is the freedom to work in other countries. British membership of the EC has given us the right to employment in other member states without needing a special permit. From northern shipyard workers, immortalised in the television soap 'Auf Wiedersehn Pet', to highly qualified southerners, the British have sought work on the Continent. About 100,000 Britons are now employed in other EC countries, including about 30,000 in Germany. The new trend has been the growth in the numbers of British entrepreneurs, managers and professionals working in Germany, France and the Benelux countries, mirroring a similar group of German, French and Dutch in Britain.[13] But until recently, the ability to work and practise elsewhere in the EC has been limited not only by language difficulties but also by the refusal by member states to recognise the professional and skill qualifications of other EC countries.

In June 1988 came a potential breakthrough. As part of the 1992 programme, the Council of Ministers agreed to a mutual recognition of diplomas and professional qualifications and the right for accountants, lawyers, engineers, psychologists and others to practise their professions in other member states. The EC Commission believes that by 1992 a professional qualification will be 'as good as a passport'. It also hopes to make similar progress on vocational training qualifications, so that skilled workers would be able to get jobs anywhere in the Community.

The consequence of removing the qualification barrier is that there is likely to be a flourishing market of mobile, skilled workers and professionals who will get jobs across the European Community. My journalist daughter and her designer husband, who live and work in France, consider it natural to look for employment on the Continent. 'Our horizons are European,' they say. Thousands of their contemporaries think the same way.

More and more Britons are also living on the Continent. There is the growing British presence on the Mediterranean coast – Europe's 'sun belt'. Since 1980, the numbers of British residents in Spain have doubled to 50,000, while they have also increased sharply in Greece and Italy. A combination of sun, sea and wine is proving irresistible to thousands of British pensioners. The British middle classes have also been snapping up second homes in France. According to one estimate, 100,000 French houses have been sold to British owners. On 17 August 1991 a *Daily Telegraph* columnist wrote: 'Merrie England is being remade in the alien corn of *la France profonde*. A dream of French rural life has taken hold of the British imagination: a population that watches *Jean de Florette* on television and reads Peter Mayle [the best selling author] in winter heads south in the summer.' An equally enticing factor is the relative cheapness of rural property in France compared to Britain. The Dordogne and Provence have long been popular. The prospect of the Channel Tunnel is now attracting growing numbers to northern France.

In the next decade the British will increasingly look on the European Community as their space to travel in, to work in and even live in. For them, as for the other Europeans, it really could become a Europe without frontiers.

## The social dimension

The founding fathers of the European Community never saw the creation of a common market as an end in itself. The Treaty of Rome specifically included a recognition that it had to lead to improvements in working conditions and living standards. Since the 1970s, even British governments have conformed to EC directives on a number of fronts, including sex equality, the rights of workers affected by transfer of undertakings and the rights of workers when employers become insolvent. When the president of the Commission, Jacques Delors, insisted that the single market will not command the support of the citizens of the Community if it is seen merely as a vehicle for increasing the markets and profits of big business, he was not only conforming to a well-established EC tradition, but also shrewdly attempting to make the single market more attractive to workers and voters.

The Social Charter, which was adopted in December 1989 with the agreement of all the member states except Britain, does not have the force of law. But it is a powerful statement of objectives which is designed to stimulate EC legislation and activity in the social field. It sets out a platform of rights to be achieved for all workers in the Community; these include freedom of movement, the right to fair remuneration, improvement of living and working conditions (especially for part-time and temporary workers), the right to social protection, freedom of association, the right to vocational training, the right to equal treatment for men and women, the right to information, consultation and participation for employees, the right to health protection and safety at work, protection of children and rights for the elderly and disabled. British Conservative governments and businesses have vehemently opposed the Social Charter. A Department of Employment memorandum in November 1989 argued that the regulatory measures envisaged by the Charter would 'hamper job creation, hinder competition within the market, damage competitiveness in world markets and put at risk all the benefits of the single market itself'. Sir Trevor Holdsworth, as chairman of the CBI, warned in June 1989 against 'a pot pourri of tired political nostrums'. Another opponent of the Charter, Tory secretary of state for employment, Michael Howard, blocked EC directives on part-time and temporary workers, quoting paragraph 2 of Article 100A of the Rome Treaty which excludes from the qualified majority voting procedure measures relating to the rights and interest of employees. Not surprisingly, the Labour Party and the trade unions strongly supported the Charter. Following the Delors argument on the need for a social dimenson, Tony Blair, as shadow employment secretary, said that 'the Social Charter has a vision of Europe in which an open market is not at the expense of the working conditions of those employed in it'. Bill Jordan, general secretary of the engineering union, argued the case for social partnership: 'If the single European market can institutionalize competition among companies, there should be no reason why it cannot institutionalize cooperation between the managers and employees who work in them'.[14] In the background is also the fear among trade

154

unionists of 'social dumping', whereby the increased competition generated by the single market drags down wages and working conditions to the lowest common denominator.

At Maastricht, the British government insisted on 'opting out' of the social protocol, covering employment rights (see Chapter 7). In the medium term, it is inconceivable that a floor of basic rights will not be introduced across the EC. Already the Social Charter has enthusiastic support among Europeans, including a majority of British voters. With the completion of the internal market, pressure from workers, students and professionals for minimum EC rights will grow. Once such a system of rights has been established, the British will increasingly look to the EC to guarantee their social rights.

As was mentioned earlier, the environmental responsibilities given to the EC under the Single European Act is strongly backed by the British people. It is widely understood that pollution by air or water does not recognise national frontiers and that an EC policy is therefore essential. The British also expect Brussels to prod a laggard government to improve standards for drinking and bathing water.

Overall, the EC's enhanced 'social dimension' is a crucial factor making the Community more attractive to the British.

### Europe of the Regions

When Britain joined the European Community, Prime Minister Edward Heath persuaded the other EC leaders to agree to set up the European Regional Development Fund, not only to help British regions but also to compensate the British for the agricultural bias of the EC's budget. One of the first British commissioners, George Thomson, introduced the Fund. But the resources allocated to it were relatively small and, in 1988, the poorer states, led by Spain, successfully insisted that the introduction of the single market should be accompanied by a major expansion of regional policies. It was agreed that the EC's structural funds (the Regional Development Fund, the Social Fund and the Agricultural Guidance Fund) should be doubled by 1993. At the same time, the resources of the Funds were to be concentrated on a limited number of objectives, above all promoting the development of regions whose GDP per head was 25 per cent below the Community average (Objective 1) and, to a lesser extent, assisting those regions seriously affected by industrial decline (Objective 2). After the Maastricht agreement which stressed the importance of the 'cohesion' of the EC, there will be pressure to increase the structural funds.

Following the 1988 reforms the proportion of the United Kingdom's population covered by EC structural funds has increased marginally from 38 per cent to 40 per cent. The United Kingdom also receives a big slice of 'Objective 2' assistance: over 38 per cent of the European Regional Development Fund's 'Objective 2' assistance goes to UK areas.

But the benefit that the British get from the EC's regional policies is limited by two factors. First, with the exception of Northern Ireland, the regions of the United Kingdom do not qualify for the far more substantial 'Objective 1' assistance which, between 1989 and 1993, will account for two-thirds of all structural funding. Second, as the British EC regional commissioner, Bruce Millan, has pointed out, the British government has been interpreting the EC's 'additionality' rule (whereby projects receiving an EC grant should be given domestic government funding in addition to and not as a substitute for existing planned public expenditure) in a way which is least helpful to the areas concerned. Even so, one important consequence of the expansion of EC structural funds is that British local councils are far more aware of the opportunities opened up by membership of the Community than ever before. One of the first questions which they now ask when planning a project is 'Is there any EC money for which we can apply?' Encouraged by the Commission, they have established direct links with Brussels. Many of them are appointing European liaison officers to advise on what is happening in the Community and liaise with Commission officials. Councillors and chief executives also keep in close contact with Euro MPs.

If the British parliament finally decides to devolve more power from Westminster to Scotland, to Wales and to the English regions this process of British involvement in Europe will intensify. UK regions are likely to follow the example of German Länder, like the Saarland and Baden Württemberg, and open permanent offices in Brussels to act as virtual embassies to the EC. They will also emulate the enthusiasm of the German Länder for an EC 'regional committee', now given official status in the Maastricht political treaty.

In the 1980s there has also been a marked increase in more informal contacts between British local councils and their counterparts in the Community. There are now over 1500 town twinnings, 70 per cent of which are with EC countries. The town-twinning movement, which started after the war to promote international reconciliation, has sometimes been criticised as an excuse for 'junketing' at the expense of the ratepayers. Judging from my own constituency experience, this charge is unfounded. Having a permanent link with, say, a town in the Ruhr, not only gives councillors the opportunity to meet and discuss matters of mutual interest with their opposite numbers; it also provides an umbrella for a wide range of cultural, sporting and educational exchanges which results in substantial involvement by local inhabitants. The sign under a British town's name-post that it is twinned with a town in Germany, France or Italy is not only becoming more and more common; it is also another symbol of Britain's growing ties with the Continent.

**A Common Culture?**
Most Europeans, including the British, think that what above all unites Europe is its culture. It depends on how culture is defined. In terms of historical, intellectual and artistic experience (see Chapter 5) and belief in democratic liberal values, the peoples of the European Community already have much in common.[15] There are also elements of popular culture which cross national boundaries, including popular music, American soap operas and European football. And, after 1992, broadcasters will be obliged to reserve a specified quota of their air time for feature films made in the European Community. But, in most respects, culture in the EC still takes on a national guise.

The complex web of habit, styles, methods and beliefs which add up to national identity is vital for all European nations, none more so than the British. Indeed, these separate national identities give European civilisation much of its vigour and strength. The idea of a common European culture does not mean that the British will have to give up eating fish and chips, drinking unchilled real ale, playing cricket or creating glorious gardens. It does, however, imply that they should be able to understand, respect and enjoy the cultures, life styles, and cuisines of other Europeans.

The ideal European, according to most Europeans including the British, is somebody who speaks a number of languages.[16] That creates a problem for the British. English is an enormous asset. Partly thanks to the Americans, it is the world's leading language in diplomacy, science and technology, international business and broadcasting. It is widely used in Europe, being one of the two official EC languages for administrative purposes. In the 1970s even the German chancellor, Helmut Schmidt, and the French president, Valéry Giscard d'Estaing, spoke together in English (in contrast to the Duke of Wellington and Marshal Blücher at the battle of Waterloo who communicated in the language of their enemy Napoleon). It is also a key business language in the EC, though German is becoming increasingly important, particularly in Central and Eastern Europe.

However the world role of English has discouraged the British from learning other languages. While other nations learn English, the British have not bothered. Their national linguistic incompetence is well documented. Even the Department of Education admits that 'we have a long way to go to catch up with other countries in the EC in terms of the numbers of languages studied, the numbers of years for which they are studied and in teaching them to pupils of all abilities'.[17]

A start has been made at improving linguistic skills.

The national curriculum requires every pupil between the age of eleven and sixteen to study a foreign language, usually French. The British are also participating in the EC's LINGUA programme which provides financial support for teachers and students and businessmen. But they still have a very long way to go, especially in the teaching of languages to people over sixteen. The House of Lords report, European Schools and Language Learning, rightly concludes: 'The attitude of British society towards modern foreign language training must change. All sectors of society must be convinced of the relevance of foreign language learning as a communications tool.'[18]

But despite the British 'hang up' over languages, exchanges at school and college level are becoming more common. Since August 1988, the Schools Unit of the Central Bureau for Educational Visits and Exchanges has set up 487 new school and college links with partner institutions in other European countries. The Central Bureau has also arranged placements for 2330 English-language assistants in EC countries during the 1990–91 academic year, while 3085 foreign-language assistants have come to work in the UK during this period.[19]

Two EC programmes have been set up to encourage higher education exchanges. The impact of COMETT, which aims to provide co-operation in technology training between higher education and business, has been relatively marginal, with about 350 British students a year going to mainland Europe. However, the second programme, ERASMUS, designed to promote student mobility across the EC, has been strikingly successful. By the end of the 1990–91 academic year over 10,000 UK students had received support from the programme, with French and German universities being the most popular. For other EC students, Britain was narrowly the most popular destination, followed by France.

In another potentially radical change, more than eighty higher institutions across the Community have agreed to recognise each other's courses. The outcome could mean, for example, a student could spend one year studying in Lancaster, another in Frankfurt and a third in Nancy and qualify for a degree wherever the final examination is taken. Fifteen British institutions have joined the scheme, importing 174 students and exporting 53 (an imbalance which is partly explained by our inferior language abilities). Looking further ahead, it is probable that there will eventually be a common school-leaving exam, on a baccalauréat model.

These developments are certain to have a significant influence on the rising generation of British students who will naturally look to the Community first for educational opportunities and then for their holidays and for future employment. For increasing numbers of British, the common aspects of European culture will inevitably grow.

### Symbols of Citizenship

Gradually, the British are becoming more accustomed to being part of the EC. In part, it is a matter of symbols. After initial hesitation, they are beginning to get used to the burgundy-coloured Euro passports. The European Community flag is now being flown, albeit somewhat cautiously, in Britain. There is growing pride when cities, like Glasgow, are awarded the resounding title of 'European City of Culture'.

Voting participation in European elections, though

rising, is little higher than in local elections. But slowly the British are getting used to the idea of having European MPs who represent them in the Community. Businesses, local authorities and pressure groups have come to see the advantage of a voice in Europe – someone who can raise issues at Strasbourg, lobby the Commission and generally act as a guide to the complexities of the EC. Many more of the British now want to extend the role of the European Parliament than want to reduce it.[20]

The British are also increasingly attracted to the idea that European institutions should guarantee their basic rights as citizens. The enthusiasm for the Social Charter and the backing for the European Court of Justice is evidence of this. The Spanish plan for a European citizenship based on freedom of movement, free choice of place of residence and the right to vote in European and local elections in the place of residence which is now incorporated in the political treaty is likely to be popular in Britain. There will also be support for the proposal for a European Ombudsman, first floated by European parliamentarians and agreed at Maastricht, to whom aggrieved Britons could turn for redress against Community institutions.

But more important than these formal symbols and rights are the impressive number and range of informal ties, economic, social and cultural, which now link us to the mainland of Europe. Almost in spite of themselves, the British are becoming *de facto* citizens of Europe.

# – 7 –

# The Conversion of the Political Class?

On 20 and 21 November 1991 the House of Commons had a two-day debate on the future of the EC before the European Council meeting at Maastricht. The media concentrated on the dramatic clash between the two Titans, ex-Prime Minister Heath and ex-Prime Minister Thatcher, on the issue of a referendum and, to a lesser extent, on the differences between the government and opposition. Only a few commentators picked up the real significance of the debate. For the first time since entry in 1973 both front benches specifically committed their parties to a constructive role for Britain within the European Community. Yet at Maastricht itself the Major government adopted a negative position. The jury is still out on the genuineness of the Conservative conversion to a positive European policy.

### Labour Becomes European
The most far-reaching change has taken place in the Labour Party. After over thirty years of ambivalence, at the end of the 1980s Labour, alongside the smaller

Liberal Democrat Party, became the main pro-European party in British politics, firmly committed to playing a positive part in the development of the European Community. In the past, Labour's attitude to the EC was at best lukewarm and at times openly hostile. In 1962, when Harold Macmillan made the first unsuccessful attempt to take Britain into the EC, the Labour Party, swayed by Hugh Gaitskell's passionate 'a thousand years of history' speech (see Chapter 1), rejected British entry on the terms negotiated by the Conservative government. In 1971, though Harold Wilson had made a fresh application for membership in the 1960s, the majority of the parliamentary Labour Party, including Wilson himself, voted against the Conservative government's accession legislation.

Although the role of Tony Benn, the born-again anti-European, was crucial during the 1970s and early 1980s, Labour's anti-Market front was always much broader than the Bennites. Part of the opposition was ideological. The left argued that the EC was a capitalist club which would block the achievement of socialism in one country. Others, such as the former cabinet minister, Douglas Jay, used more straightforward economic arguments. The Common Market, according to Jay, would mean 'higher food prices, a less favourable balance in manufactured goods, and a Budget payment'.[1] Peter Shore, another distinguished cabinet minister, stressed more profound issues of national identity. The EC, in Shore's eyes, would inevitably be an inward-looking, Continental bloc, alien to British values and attitudes. Britain's links ought rather to be with the United States and the Commonwealth. It was Shore who once said: 'There are more people of European origin outside the continent of Europe than in the EC and they all speak English.' There is no doubt that there was also a strong streak of old-fashioned 'offshore' chauvinism in Labour's anti-Europeanism. The left-winger, Eric Heffer, admitted as much when he wrote that the party had its share of Little Englanders 'who suffer from the delusion that civilisation ends at Dover'.[2]

Throughout the 1970s, Europe remained a divisive issue for the Labour Party. The 1975 referendum which confirmed British membership was at least in part a device for keeping the party together. But it failed to heal the divisions. When in 1977 the House of Commons voted on direct elections to the European Parliament, 126 Labour MPs voted in favour and 126 against, an indication of the depth and seriousness of the split over the EC. As the party swung to the left after its 1979 election defeat, it changed its position of qualified acceptance to one of outright rejection. The 1980 motion calling for withdrawal was a Bennite initiative, part of a general repudiation of the Wilson/Callaghan years. Withdrawal became one of the key issues in Labour's civil war and a major cause of the SDP breakaway which so weakened the Labour Party in the early 1980s. The Labour Party fought the June 1983 election, in which it was so decisively defeated, on a pledge to take Britain out of the EC 'well within the lifetime of a Labour government'. Yet, by the 1989 Euro-elections, it had become enthusiastically pro-European.

Why did Labour change its position over Europe so dramatically? The short answer is that it became convinced, in the words of one perceptive observer, 'that the EC framework could be used to implement progressive policies'.[3] It is instructive to chart this shift in terms of individual personalities. Three people are mainly responsible for Labour's conversion – Neil Kinnock, Margaret Thatcher and Jacques Delors.

Immediately after the 1983 defeat, Neil Kinnock, who was elected leader at the party conference later that year, called for a reconsideration of the withdrawal policy. Between 1983 and 1987, he gradually guided the party towards a position of conditional acceptance. Then after Labour's third successive defeat in 1987, Kinnock moved the party decisively in support of the European Community. Like his mentor and predecessor, Michael Foot, Neil Kinnock had been an opponent of the EC. Now he became a pro-European convert. What persuaded him to change his mind?

Of course, as a good party leader, he was concerned with political advantage. Like the majority of his colleagues, he had concluded in 1983 that Labour's anti-Europeanism was a vote loser. After 1987, Mrs Thatcher's negative stance on European issues and fresh poll evidence of a more favourable attitude to the EC by a growing section of the electorate exposed a weak flank which the Labour Party was understandably eager to exploit. But Labour's new Europeanism goes well beyond mere electoral opportunism. As a Welshman, Neil Kinnock was never a 'Little Englander'. His opposition to the EC had been based not on xenophobia but on the judgement that, because Britain had not been an original member of the Community, its rules worked against British interests. By 1983, it had become clear to him that withdrawal was not a feasible option. Talk of withdrawal was, in his view, both 'politically romantic and economically self-defeating'. As he told a meeting of junior front bench spokesmen in 1984, the sensible course was not to criticise ineffectively from the sidelines but to participate fully in the development of the EC.

As leader, Neil Kinnock made it a priority to build up relationships with Continental socialists. He was prominent not only in the work of the Socialist International but also in that of the Confederation of the Socialist Parties of the EC. At a personal level, he got to know European statesmen and party leaders such as Willy Brandt, Hans Jochen Vogel, Felipe Gonzalez, Michel Rocard and Bettino Craxi. An important milestone was his involvement, at the invitation of Gonzalez, in the 1985 Spanish referendum campaign on NATO membership.

At a party level, co-operation has been greatly improved. Over the last five years the Labour Party has held joint seminars with the German Social Democrats (SPD) and the French Socialists (PS). In 1989 Labour broke new ground by fighting the European elections on a joint manifesto with other European parties. Peter Shore has even complained that the party is suffering from 'total immersion in Europe'.[4]

The party's long spell in opposition also gave it time to reflect how much the world had changed. Labour's leaders drew appropriate conclusions from the failure of President François Mitterrand's 'Keynesianism in one country' experiment in France in 1981–3. As a Fabian author put it, 'To seek to implement policies without the fullest reference to what is happening beyond national frontiers . . . is to invite disaster, as the French discovered.'[5] Neil Kinnock's answer was to co-ordinate British economic policies with other European countries, to work for 'a common strategy for expansion'.[6]

The Labour leadership also noted the higher social

standards in other European countries and how much the progressive thinking and action on the environment and on social issues came not from London but from Brussels. Kinnock gave strong support to the idea that 'the social dimension of the Single Market must be central to the prospectus and to the practice of the European Community'.[7] By the end of the 1980s, it had become clear Europe was a vital ingredient in Labour's revisionism.

The party's shift on the EC is well illustrated by the initiative which it took on British membership of the exchange rate mechanism (ERM). While Mrs Thatcher dragged her feet over Britain joining the ERM through 1988 and 1989, it became the cornerstone of Labour's anti-inflation policy. John Smith, as shadow chancellor and a committed supporter of the EC, argued that, because the ERM would stabilise the UK exchange rate, it would provide a valuable counter inflationary discipline. Firms which were unable to rely on a depreciating currency to pass on increased costs would think twice before conceding inflationary wage demands. Through its ERM policy, Labour attempted to solve an old British problem by fitting it into a new European framework. It also paved the way for its later support in principle for economic and monetary union (EMU).

In the autumn of 1989, John Smith, accompanied by Gordon Brown, then shadow chief secretary, and with the full backing of Neil Kinnock, made a successful tour of a number of key European cities, including Paris, Brussels, Frankfurt and Bonn. This trip had two purposes. The first was to refine Labour's position on the ERM and to develop its thinking on the EMU debate. The second was to send a message to European leaders about Labour's new Europeanism. *The Guardian* commented on 20 October 1989: 'Western European governments are realising not only that Labour is back in political business at home, but that a potential Labour government will be a European force with which they can do business on a wider EC stage.'

Mrs Thatcher's role in the Labour Party's change was crucial. Her hostility to the EC provided Labour with a key electoral opportunity. The inadequacies of her government, especially in the social field, threw into relief the attractions of the EC. Most important of all, the failure of Mrs Thatcher's European policy revealed the shortcomings of British Gaullism. Mrs Thatcher's demonstration of how not to do it helped persuade the Labour Party that it could only be successful if it was wholeheartedly committed to the EC. George Robertson, speaking as Labour's European spokesman, argued in a European debate in November 1989:

> Her approach is nit-picking, carping and mean spirited. We are repeatedly marginalized and ignored. The vote on the Social Charter . . . will leave Britain isolated. . . . It is again stark evidence of the denial to the British people of the reasonable employment standards that they might expect from the completion of the Single Market.[8]

Labour's European education was completed by the new direction which Jacques Delors' presidency of the European Commission gave to the EC. Jacques Delors' insistence on the social dimension of the single market and his almost evangelical support of the Social Charter was much admired by the British labour movement. His address to the TUC at Bournemouth in 1988, which received three standing ovations, is rightly regarded as

a key event in Labour's conversion. Delors promised
delegates:

> First, the establishment of the platform of guaran-
> teed social rights. . . . Second, the creation of a
> statute for European companies which would
> include the participation of workers and their
> representatives . . . third, the extension of all work-
> ers of the right to life-long education in a changing
> society.

Delors' eloquent speech was followed a month later by
an equally rousing address by Neil Kinnock to the
Labour Party conference, in which he committed the
party to a 'Social Europe'.

The leadership's new line on Europe went through
virtually unchallenged. The trade unions, as was
described in the previous chapter, had already been
converted. Inside the parliamentary party, a change of
generations helped shift the climate of opinion. It is
remarkable how, almost without exception, all the
younger Labour MPs were pro EC and the rising stars
of the shadow cabinet were enthusiastically European.
Even former anti-Europeans changed their minds.
Gerald Kaufman, as Labour's Shadow Foreign Secretary, who originally opposed membership of the EC
on the grounds of sovereignty, argued that, in a world
of super trade blocs, a medium-sized economic power
like Britain cannot hope to survive on its own. There
were also some notable left-wing converts, including
Brian Sedgemore who believed that changes in the
organisation of international capital have undermined
the argument for socialism in one country. The anti-
marketeers had been reduced to a small group of older

MPs who now had little influence on the direction of policy. Labour's support for the EC was officially signalled in its far-reaching policy review document *Meet the Challenge, Make the Change*, published in May 1989. The review has rightly been described as Labour's Bad Godesberg because, like the German Social Democrat party's new programme forty years before, it committed the party to a modernised approach. A vital element in the party's revisionism and in its increasingly popular appeal was its new commitment to Europe. The review argued for a positive agenda: 'We want the British people to get the best from the European Community'. Labour had become European.

### The 1989 European Election – A Turning Point

In retrospect, the 1989 European election was far more significant than it seemed to most political commentators at the time. It was not only the first occasion for fifteen years that Labour had beaten the Conservatives in a national election. It was not merely the beginning of the end for Mrs Thatcher. In the longer term, the most important message of all was that it demonstrated conclusively that the anti-European card was no longer effective in British politics.

The media could be forgiven for not paying too much attention to the European elections. The previous two British Euro elections had been virtual non-events. In 1979, the first direct election had merely underlined the victory which Mrs Thatcher had achieved in the general election a month earlier, while in 1984, the Conservatives finished comfortably ahead of Labour who were only just beginning to recover from the electoral catastrophe of 1983. In both elections turn-out at 32 per cent was abysmally low and in so far as there were issues at all these were national rather than European. In contrast, European questions played a key role in the 1989 election. Throughout much of 1989, Mrs Thatcher's attacks on plans for European integration in general and on Jacques Delors in particular, dominated the headlines. Mrs Thatcher's opposition to the Delors report on economic and monetary union, to the Social Charter and to other EC initiatives, including the LINGUA programme, all ensured that the European elections would be at least in part about Mrs Thatcher's handling of European matters.

An added bonus for Labour was that Mrs Thatcher's posture on the EC split the Conservative Party. It not only infuriated Conservative MEPs and Euro enthusiasts at Westminster like the former prime minister, Edward Heath; more ominously for Mrs Thatcher, it gave Michael Heseltine, who had resigned from her cabinet and was a potential rival for her crown, an issue on which to challenge her. The month before the European election he chose to publish a book in favour of European integration.

Most dangerous of all, the question of British membership of the European exchange rate mechanism divided the Thatcher cabinet. While Mrs Thatcher was vehemently opposed, both the chancellor of the exchequer, Nigel Lawson, and the foreign secretary, Sir Geoffrey Howe, were in favour of early membership. In March 1988 Mrs Thatcher openly denounced Lawson's policy of unofficially shadowing the Deutschmark when she told the Commons, 'There is no way in which one can buck the market'. The semi-public row over ERM membership continued to attract damaging media attention in the months leading up to the June 1989 election.

Labour went into the Euro elections in good heart. At a domestic level, the Conservatives were becoming increasingly unpopular, particularly over their handling of the economy and the national health service. The publication of the policy review at the end of May highlighted Labour's transformation as an acceptable alternative. Equally important, the party's pro-EC stance put it in a strong position to exploit Conservative disarray over Europe.

The Labour campaign, skilfully co-ordinated by the former anti-marketeer Bryan Gould, sensibly used the tenth anniversary of Mrs Thatcher's accession to power to launch an attack on the government's domestic record, particularly on the economy and the health service. But it also highlighted the costs to the voters of the government's opposition to the Social Charter and its feet-dragging over EC environmental standards. Labour convincingly argued that a more constructive European approach could bring tangible social benefits to the British people, 'an upward harmonisation of all standards across the Community to the highest possible levels'.

The Conservatives mistakenly fought a purely negative campaign. They tried unsuccessfully to portray Labour as split over Europe and repeated *ad nauseam* Thatcherite propaganda against European integration. 'We did not join Europe to be swallowed up in some bureaucratic conglomerate, where it's Euro-this and Euro-that and forget about being British or French or Italian or Spanish,' thundered Mrs Thatcher. In the final week, the Conservatives put up posters which sustained the 'Euro-bashing' theme. 'Stay at home on 15 June and

173

you'll live on a diet of Brussels' ran the crudely anti-European slogan.

The result was a kick in the teeth for the Tories and a significant boost for Labour. The Conservatives lost thirteen seats, while their share of the vote at 34.7 per cent was their lowest at any election since the beginning of universal suffrage. Labour broke the crucial 40 per cent barrier and increased its representation in the European parliament to forty-five seats, thus forming the biggest block in the Socialist group. The other winner was the Green Party which dramatically increased its proportion from 0.6 per cent to 14.9 per cent of the vote.

The chief importance of the 1989 election, however, was what it revealed about British attitudes to the EC. Even though the turn out at 37 per cent of the vote was still the lowest in the EC, the election result showed that the British now wanted their government to take a more positive line on Europe. Mrs Thatcher had played the anti-European card and had been decisively defeated. As Peter Jenkins wrote in *The Independent*, 'Her kind of chauvinism is plainly out of fashion'.[9] The emphasis of Labour and the Green Party on seeking solutions for national problems within a European framework was shown to be far more to the electorate's liking. In 1989, far more decisively than at the 1975 referendum, the British voted for a European future.

### Margaret Thatcher's Downfall over Europe

Queen Mary Tudor is reputed to have said on being told about the loss of Calais: 'When I am dead and opened, you shall find "Calais" lying in my heart.' According to Nicholas Ridley, 'When Mrs Thatcher is dead and opened, it will be those three letters "ERM" that will be lying in her heart.'[10] However, though the question of the ERM has a strong claim, it was the general issue of Europe which precipitated her downfall.

The political importance of the division over British membership of the ERM was that it poisoned the prime minister's relations with the two most powerful figures in her cabinet – Nigel Lawson and Sir Geoffrey Howe. In July 1989 before the European Summit at Madrid, they persuaded Mrs Thatcher to commit Britain to join the ERM. Under their pressure, she agreed to make such a commitment, though it was hedged around with conditions – the so-called Madrid conditions. Sir Geoffrey Howe later explained what happened: 'The so-called Madrid conditions came into existence only after the then Chancellor and myself as Foreign Secretary made it clear that we could not continue in office unless a specific commitment to join the ERM was made.'[11]

Mrs Thatcher did not forgive her two cabinet colleagues for forcing her to give way. A month later she demoted Howe by moving him out of the foreign office and making him leader of the House. In October 1989, she made little effort to retain Nigel Lawson as chancellor when he resigned over her reappointment of Alan Walters as her economic adviser. Lawson and Howe who previously had been among Mrs Thatcher's strongest supporters now became implacable enemies.

However, it was not the ERM issue which led to Howe's resignation in November 1990 and to his bitter attack on Mrs Thatcher in his House of Commons' resignation speech. For on 2 October, just before the Conservative Party conference, Britain had joined the ERM. Rather, it was exasperation with Mrs Thatcher's attitude to the European Community in general and to

European Monetary Union in particular. When on her return from Rome Mrs Thatcher made her statement to the Commons on 30 October 1990 (see Chapter 4), I watched Sir Geoffrey Howe sitting next to her on the government front bench. Though Sir Geoffrey normally has more than his share of lawyer's caution, his facial expression that fateful afternoon revealed his dismay at Mrs Thatcher's inflammatory anti-European responses to questions. He visibly winced when, in referring to Jacques Delors' views on the future of the EC, she stridently cried 'No, No, No'. Sir Geoffrey had had enough and two days later he resigned, saying that he was 'deeply anxious that the mood you have struck . . . will make it more difficult for Britain to hold and retain a position of influence in this vital debate'.[12]

It was Sir Geoffrey's resignation speech on 13 November which set in motion the train of events which led to Mrs Thatcher's fall. Howe's damning charge against Mrs Thatcher was that her European policy was 'running increasingly serious risks for the future of our nation' and he warned that if the government detached itself 'from the middle ground of Europe' the effects would be 'incalculable and very hard to correct'. The atmosphere in the chamber and in the lobbies afterwards was electric. It was clear that the impact on Conservative MPs of Sir Geoffrey's devastating indictment of Mrs Thatcher's European policy was considerable. Meeting Michael Heseltine by chance at the entrance to the chamber later that evening, I remarked to him: 'The question now is not whether Heseltine will run but whether Thatcher will survive.' He only smiled in reply but he looked like a cat who had swallowed the cream.

Michael Heseltine had been hesitating over whether

or not to run against Mrs Thatcher in the leadership election. The previous October, a pro-European back-bencher, Sir Anthony Meyer, had been put up as a stalking horse and received thirty-three votes with twenty-seven abstentions. Heseltine had to fare better than that if he were to risk putting his hat in the ring. Now Sir Geoffrey's speech gave him the opportunity which he sought and the next day he declared his candidature, citing Mrs Thatcher's handling of Europe as the main reason for his challenge, though cleverly he also promised 'a fundamental review of the poll tax', the hugely unpopular local government tax.

There were a number of reasons why 152 Tory MPs voted against Mrs Thatcher on the first ballot of the Tory leadership election and why her cabinet colleagues then persuaded her to stand down. The overriding one was survival, naturally enough a vital matter for politi-cians. The Tory MPs wanted to save their seats, so they ditched Mrs Thatcher. But it was Mrs Thatcher's split with the majority of her cabinet colleagues and the majority of Conservative MPs over the European Com-munity which undermined her authority and provided the main pretext for the challenge to her. It was Europe which brought Mrs Thatcher down.

## John Major's Change of Style

John Major, who became prime minister on 28 Novem-ber 1990 after his victory in the second ballot, did not have particularly pronounced views on the EC, either for or against. He had risen effortlessly at the court of 'Queen Margaret', a likeable, competent technocrat who could be relied upon to support her views. The only straw in the wind was that, when chancellor of the exchequer, he had finally persuaded Mrs Thatcher to agree that Britain should join the ERM.

Later John Major made much of the fact that, like Neil Kinnock, he was of the new generation, a generation for which Europe was a 'cause of political inspiration'. Certainly it was an advantage that Major had not been involved in the bruising debates of the 1960s and 1970s and could therefore consider European issues less viscerally and more on their merits.

The crucial point, however, was that Mrs Thatcher's strident anti-Europeanism was simply not viable, either for the Conservative Party or for the nation as a whole. It had already split the Tories and risked isolating Britain in the European Community. If Major was to have a chance at the general election, he had, however cautiously, to shift ground on Europe.

Shrewdly, Major chose to make his first speech on Europe at the Konrad Adenauer Foundation, the Christian Democrat (CDU) think-tank in Bonn, on 11 March 1991. He began his address by paying a warm tribute to the German chancellor, Helmut Kohl, with whom Mrs Thatcher had had such glacial relations. He also spoke approvingly of the 'social market' tradition of the CDU, another break with Thatcherism. Above all, he emphasised his government's attachment to the European Community. 'My aims for Britain in the Community could be simply stated,' said Major, 'I want us to be where we belong. At the very heart of Europe, working with our partners in building the future.'

In his Bonn speech, the new prime minister set out the familiar Conservative objections to an 'imposed' single currency. But, in marked contrast to Mrs Thatcher, he also gave a hint of a willingness to compromise. He said that he was confident that the Intergovernmental Conferences would be able to work out arrangements which protected the right of a future British parliament to make a decision on a single currency later. In other words, if her Community partners were prepared to wait for a British commitment on a single currency, then Britain would allow economic and monetary union to go ahead.

Later, on 26 June 1991, in a speech to the Commons, the foreign secretary, Douglas Hurd, made it clear the government was also seeking to sign an agreement over political union. 'We are working for agreement,' said Hurd. He went on: 'We cannot dictate what our children will make of the Community, but I am sure that we must leave them in a position where they can effectively influence the shape of Europe.' Replying directly to a critical speech by Mrs Thatcher, he warned: 'History would deal harshly with us if we retreated into some form of querulous isolation, worried always at the prospect of being outwitted by clever foreigners and acting always as a brake on the ideas of others without putting forward ideas of our own.'

By the end of 1991 a post-Thatcher line on the EC was being cautiously evolved by the new Conservative leadership. But though the Major government had abandoned the isolation of Mrs Thatcher, it was very slow indeed in coming forward with constructive ideas of its own. One commentator wrote: 'The prime minister continues to give the impression of backing into Europe somewhat in the manner of a gatecrasher entering a party by pretending he is going home'.[13] The problem for Major in the run-up to Maastricht was that his hesitant Europeanism was too much for some of his highly vocal Conservative critics, while it risked being too little either to maximise British influence or secure British interests in the European Community.

## 'Game, Set and Match' at Maastricht

John Major proclaimed that the result of the European Council meeting at Maastricht on 9 and 10 December 1991 was 'game, set and match for Britain'. In contrast, opposition critics argued that, as a consequence of his negotiating tactics, Britain had been left isolated. Neil Kinnock summed up the Labour case in the Commons in the two day Commons debate following Maastricht: 'A Prime Minister who said that he wanted Britain at the heart of Europe spent his whole time at the Council getting two escape clauses.'[14]

It is clear that Major's overriding objective at Maastricht was to obtain an agreement which he could sell to Conservative anti-Europeans, including Mrs Thatcher. The main purpose of the two opt out clauses obtained by Major was to prevent a split in Tory ranks. But, in giving priority to pacifying his party, he both reduced British influence on the final shape of the Maastricht agreement and left Britain isolated in the European Community.

With respect to a single currency, the weakness of making the right to opt out the primary bargaining objective was that Britain was then unable to influence other, more important decisions on economic and monetary union. The one real surprise at the Maastricht meeting, and the main achievement of the French negotiators, was the fixing of a final date for the beginning of the third stage on 1 January 1999. The British government had, with some justice, argued against such a fixed date but, because the whole of Britain's credit had been used up in securing the right to opt out, British negotiators were unable to affect the crucial decision on timing.

It is no secret that most Conservative ministers, including John Major, want Britain ultimately to be in a position to join a single currency. But by going for an opt out clause the Major government created uncertainty – uncertainty about the intentions of foreign investors and inward investment, uncertainty about domestic investment in this country and uncertainty in the City about whether it will retain its predominant position. A British decision to accept the objective of a single currency would have lent credibility to anti-inflation policies, would have provided an economic and monetary environment conducive to change and, above all, would have shown that Britain was serious about economic and monetary union.

The second British 'opt out' was the refusal to agree to a social chapter being included in the political treaty and subsequent exclusion from the social protocol agreed at Maastricht by the other eleven members. John Major's tactics can be criticised on two grounds. First, it appeared to be conceding that British employees, alone amongst the eleven members of the EC, should not enjoy minimum social and labour market arrangements and that Britain should become the 'sweat-shop' of Europe. Secondly, it went some way towards creating a two-tier Europe, with Britain in the second tier. Above all, it left the British once again isolated in the European Community.

Jacques Delors' comment on British tactics at Maastricht was astringent: 'When I look back at Maastricht, I must say that the British problem still remains with us, both psychologically and politically. In the positions defended by John Major and Douglas Hurd, I found the same principles that guided the attitudes of Mrs Thatcher. The style is different, but I found the same fears.'[15]

### Europeanisation of British Politics

Europe featured little in the 1992 general election. The Conservatives, who in their manifesto inaccurately claimed that they had ensured that 'Britain is at the heart of Europe', kept quiet about the EC for fear of stirring up the Thatcherites. The Labour Party, which in their manifesto promised to promote Britain 'out of the European second division', were uncertain about the electoral appeal of their new found Europeanism. Only Paddy Ashdown, leader of the Liberal Democrats, devoted any campaigning time to the issue. As if to prove the Continent existed, he boarded a channel ferry to make an electioneering speech in France. The media, which had fully reported the debate leading up to Maastricht, paid little attention to Britain's future in Europe. An Italian journalist commented: 'If Britons look carefully at a map, just below the British Isles they may notice a bulky mass of land. It is populated by a variety of different peoples, who have only one thing in common in the course of a British election campaign: they are totally forgotten by the British.'[16]

Yet, in the 1990s, such an attitude is no longer viable. Most MPs, of whatever party, cannot conceive of a future for this country outside the European Community. Most voters do not want Britain to be left out of European developments. Above all, the logic of an ever-closer involvement with the EC impels a more constructive approach. Inevitably, British politics will become Europeanised.

Already the Bagehot column in *The Economist* has noted a change in the habits of ministers and civil servants:

> What is happening is a string of incremental changes in the lives of Her Majesty's ministers and their minions. Britain is starting to experience what other Community countries have been getting used to for decades – the creation of a new EC-wide ruling class. They are the ministers who see more of airport lounges and their European colleagues than they do of the Commons tea rooms and their own backbenchers. They are the civil servants who have learnt Community law and fluent French.[17]

It is noticeable how both Labour and Conservative parties are eager to demonstrate their links with their corresponding parties on the mainland. In Berlin, Neil Kinnock addressed the Confederation of European Socialists. In Bonn, John Major spoke at the head-quarters of the CDU. The handshakes with Chancellor Kohl, President Mitterrand or Prime Minister Gonzalez help to underline the European credentials of British political leaders.

Even today, the political agenda is partly shaped by European comparisons. When the Labour party criticises the unemployment or training records of the Conservative government, it relates its attack to what is happening in other EC countries. When the Conservative government boasts about its inflation record, it measures its progress against the German rate. Over the next decade, British politicians will express their differences in as much a European as in a national context. Increasingly it is accepted by both main parties that some policies, for example environmental protection, have to be on a Community basis. With the development of economic and monetary union and closer political union, debates about the economy, defence or foreign policy will be as much about whether the correct European policy is being adopted as about divergences in national policy. The argument will also be about which policies should be decided at European level. Even now Conservatives emphasise the importance of competition within a single EC market, while Labour leaders stress the need for European-wide social protection.

Looking ahead, the European Parliament will inevitably increase in power and influence. This will not only have an impact on the role of the Westminster Parliament but will also encourage many of the ablest and most ambitious politicians to make a career in Europe. It will also require British political parties to give priority to building common political platforms with sister parties on the Continent.

In these ways, British politics will become more European in style, method and content. The Europeanisation of our political life will become extensive.

# Conclusion: At the Heart of Europe

The nineteenth-century French statesman and historian, Adolphe Thiers, when asked to comment on British policy or history, would reply: 'but would it not have been sufficient to say that England is an island?'[1] For too long the British have been reluctant Europeans. Their reluctance stems from a deep-seated insularity, an 'offshore' mentality and a strong sense of national identity. Their patriotism, which goes back at least as far as the Tudors, has helped this country survive two world wars. But it also makes them suspicious and sometimes contemptuous of the Continentals.

The British belief that Britain is 'no ordinary country' has been shaped by an exceptional historical experience. Its parliament, constitutional development and system of law has set Britain apart from the Continent. With command of the seas, it became a world empire, ruling over a quarter of the globe. It was a victor in the 1914–18 and 1939–45 wars. In 1940, the British stood proudly alone against Hitler. Unlike the other eleven members of the EC, they have not experienced serious military defeat, occupation, civil war or revolution for at least two hundred years.

**From Reluctance to Acceptance**
Yet, in the post-war world, history has been a poor guide. Sadly a whole generation of British political leaders were seduced by 'an idea' of Britain which was an anachronism. At a time when a decline in power and a shift of interests argued strongly for British participation in European integration, they remained ambivalant about being too closely involved with those whom they saw as unreliable Continentals. As a consequence, the British squandered crucial opportunities in Europe – over the Schuman Plan in 1950, over the Common Market in 1955–57 and over the European Monetary System in the late 1970s and 1980s. It was a classic failure of political leadership.

However, our attempt to stand aloof from Continental developments could never work. Geographically, Britain is a group of islands off the mainland of Europe. Historically and culturally, it has always been closely linked to the Continent. Strategically what happens there is bound to be a vital British interest. Economically Britain cannot afford to be excluded from a European bloc which includes Germany. It is a medium-sized, post-imperial European power, tied to the Continent not only by the umbilical cord of geography, history and culture but also by the vital necessities of economics, politics and security.

The British people are now waking up to this inescapable fact. Since 1989 there has been sustained majority support for the Community. Although there are still doubts about the issue of sovereignty, there is also strong backing for many aspects of European integration, especially the Social Charter and common environmental policies. Above all, the British do not want to be left out of future developments in Europe.

186

# Conclusion

One reason is that the British are already becoming *de facto* citizens of Europe. Consumers buy Continental goods. Workers' jobs depend on success in European markets. They travel, take holidays, increasingly work and even live on the mainland. Europe is becoming a British space.

A shift is also taking place in the political class. The most far-reaching change has taken place in the Labour Party. After thirty years in which Labour's attitude to the EC was at best lukewarm and at times openly hostile, at the end of the 1980s Labour became the main pro-European party in British politics, firmly committed to playing a positive part in the development of the EC. With the downfall of Mrs Thatcher, the Conservatives, under John Major, were in a strong position to move government policy in a more constructive direction. Major began promisingly in March 1991 when he said in Bonn: 'I want us to be where we belong. At the very heart of Europe, working with out partners in building the future.' But, though his tone was a welcome change from his predecessor's strident English nationalism, his attitude in the run up to the Maastricht European Council meeting remained negative. Instead of emphasizing the opportunities opened up by European integration, he attempted to portray himself as a doughty defender of a Britain besieged by hordes of marauding Continentals. He failed to explain that in the modern world the most effective way a medium sized nation can exert influence is through joining together with others. At Maastricht, the result of John Major's narrow negotiating strategy was to leave Britain isolated and unable to influence vital developments in the EC.

But, over the next decade, a negative stance will no longer be viable. The logic of an ever-closer involvement with the European Community, combined with pressure from an increasingly pragmatic electorate, will impel a more constructive approach by British politicians. Below I set out a positive agenda for the re-elected Major government.

## A New Style in Europe

The Major government needs to begin by becoming more *communautaire*; it must adopt a style which is more consistent with playing a positive role in the EC.[2]

Being a member of the Community involves a continuous process of negotiation and compromise. It is not a 'them and us' situation, with the British fighting bravely alone against hostile Europeans. If the European Council is always portrayed as a battleground, it not only encourages public hostility to the Community but also infuriates other members of the EC. The British will not make the most of their potential influence inside Europe unless they convince their partners that they are working with rather than against them. Every deal should be seen as a victory but let it be a victory for the Community as well as for Britain. Major's triumphalist claim after Maastricht − 'game, set and match for Britain' − was not only at variance with the facts; it was a poor way to win friends in Europe.

Britain also needs to build relationships with the Community, especially with France and Germany. Of course, the Franco-German partnership will continue to be crucial for the EC. But there ought also to be a triangular relationship between Britain, Germany and France as well. The British and the Germans share the view that the EC should be widened in terms of membership, particularly in Central and Eastern Europe, and be open to the outside world. France and Britain have security interests in common, including the possession of nuclear weapons. And, with a more powerful Germany, France may wish to have Britain as an additional co-partner. Britain must also take more seriously its relations with the southern member states, particularly Italy and Spain.

In his 1989 Granada lecture, the British commissioner, Sir Leon Brittan, suggested that, if Britain objects to a proposal, it is sometimes more sensible to adopt a 'yes but' approach and then seek to improve it by amendment. As Sir Leon pointed out, in this way Britain would stand a better chance of achieving a more acceptable solution.

Britain must become more pro-active. France and Germany are much more effective than Britain in putting forward ideas which subsequently become Community policy. Leon Brittan's advice to the British is: 'Stop asking: What is hitting us from Brussels and what can we do about it? Start asking: Is there anything that we want and how can we persuade Brussels to adopt it?'[3] The Conservative government, which assumes the Presidency of the European Council from July to December 1992, has an unrivalled opportunity to launch some positive initiatives.

### Designers as well as Craftsmen
Mrs Thatcher saw Britain as the European Community's sheet anchor, attempting to stem the tide of integration. Douglas Hurd has suggested that the British should be 'the craftsmen rather than the visionaries of Europe'.[4] Hurd's formulation is preferable to Mrs Thatcher's, in that it at least envisages them playing an active part in shaping the EC's future. But though there is clearly a role for their traditional pragmatic virtues,

189

the British should be designers as well as craftsmen, with constructive European aims of their own. Here is my list of objectives for the British Presidency and beyond. Britain should stop procrastinating and back the principle of economic and monetary union. Accepting the prospect of a single currency would help promote the process of economic convergence by providing a strong economic and monetary framework within which to adapt our economy. The advantages to be derived from EMU – the abolition of transaction costs, the elimination of exchange rate instability, and the achievement of a stable environment for growth – far outweigh the disadvantages.

Britain should strongly support the concept of a 'Social Europe'. If the single market is to retain the support of the people of the Community, it has also to provide a minimum level of social protection across the EC. Obviously if it is set too high, it could undermine the competitive position of poorer regions. But it is essential that employees as well as employers feel they have a stake in the Single European Market. Britain should also continue to support other measures, including regional policies, to improve the social cohesion of the Community.

The Conservative government should back those who argue for greater accountability. They have justly prided themselves on their commitment to parliamentary democracy. But it is not possible to 'plug' the democratic deficit merely by increasing the involvement of national parliaments. European institutions can only be called to account by increasing the powers of the European Parliament.

The EC must be made more accessible to its citizens.[5] That means supporting measures to ease travel restrictions, promoting exchanges and educational, cultural and language programmes, and devising an effective and speedy European complaints system. It also means guaranteeing human rights on a European basis.

Britain must back common foreign and security policies. The best way to maximise British influence in the world is to make the EC as a whole more influential.

The British government must uphold the idea of an 'open Europe'. This implies the widening of the EC to accept as many European nations as possible, including the former Soviet bloc countries of Eastern and Central Europe. It implies support for an open world trading system. It implies the provision of aid to developing countries and opening EC markets to their goods.

## Sustaining Labour's EC Commitment

Despite its fourth successive defeat at the April 1992 general election, the Labour Party must sustain its new commitment to the European Community. A switch back to outright opposition or even to scepticism would lack any political credibility. It would cut Labour off from constructive dialogue with other European Community sister parties. Above all, it would run against the grain of underlying developments which are binding Britain to the mainland of Europe.

A crucial issue in Labour's leadership election following Neil Kinnock's resignation has been the differing attitudes of the candidates towards Britain's relationship with the European Community. Bryan Gould has long been a Euro-sceptic, believing that the ERM is an uncomfortable straightjacket for the British economy and that a single currency could be a recipe for deflation. In contrast, John Smith has been a convinced European

191

for more than thirty years and is firmly committed to British membership of the ERM and a supporter of the principle of a European single currency.

There may well be an argument for a devaluation of sterling as part of an agreed realignment with the ERM. When the Conservative government belatedly took Britain into the ERM in October 1990, I said in the House of Commons that we had joined 'at the wrong time, for the wrong reason and at the wrong rate'. But it would be foolish for the Labour Party to confuse a technical debate about the value of the exchange rate with an illusory belief that the British economy can be run independently of what happens on the Continent. Britian cannot now withdraw from the ERM or, if it goes ahead, opt out of a single currency.

There is no salvation for Labour as an anti-European or reluctant European party. It must continue to set its domestic policies, social and environmental as well as economic, within a European framework. It must continue to develop a strategy for Europe, including the strengthening of the European Parliament. Labour's future, like that of Britan, lies in the European Community.


## A Modern Patriotism

Pride in one's country will, and indeed should, remain a powerful force in Britain. But we need to define a modern version of patriotism which is more in keeping with playing a positive role in the EC.[6] It must be based on a realistic assessment of Britain's position in the world. It must look forwards rather than back. And it must be more generous and less xenophobic.

It should be based on the qualities which the Continentals still admire in the British – the support for parliamentary democracy, the commitment to individual freedom, and the sense of 'fair play'.

It would look to the thinkers, artists and doers as well as the wealth creators for role models. The British are right to be proud of the achievement of their scientists, designers, engineers, doctors, nurses, writers, musicians, actors, broadcasters and athletes, amongst others.

It would applaud enterprise but at the same time give high priority to caring for others. We should rejoice in the successes of British industry. But we should be equally proud of a good National Health Service, an effective education system, a decent transport network and clean and tidy streets.

It would build on the advantage of speaking the world's international language. It would invest in the immense global reputation and prestige of the BBC. It would develop our great universities as European centres of learning.

Last but not least, it would take pride in British involvement on the European mainland. On the Continent, the skills of British diplomatic negotiators and the professionalism of the armed forces are much admired. Their European friends now want the British to forget their anachronistic ideas about sovereignty and draw on their democratic commitment and parliamentary experience to help strengthen EC institutions, particularly the European Parliament. Above all, they want the British to become participating Europeans. It is indeed time for Britain to join Europe.

# Notes

## Introduction

1 Stephen George, *An Awkward Partner*, Oxford, Oxford University Press 1990.

2 *Eurobarometer*, European Commission, December 1990.

3 *Sunday Telegraph*, 9 December 1990 and *Daily Telegraph*, 10 December 1990; ICM/*Today* poll, 1 June 1991.

4 Sofres-AGB/*The European*, June 1991 (quoted in the *Eurobrits* GGT Advertising Ltd, November 1991).

## 1 'A Thousand Years of History'

1 Susan Briggs, *Keeping Smiling Through*, London, Weidenfeld & Nicolson 1975, p. 61.

2 Denis Healey, *The Time of My Life*, London, Michael Joseph 1989, p. 211.

3 Philip M. Williams, *Hugh Gaitskell*, London, Jonathan Cape 1979, pp. 734–5.

4 *Der Spiegel*, 30 March 1990 (quoted by William Wallace, 'Foreign Policy and National Identity', *International Affairs*, Vol 67 No. 1 January 1991).

5 Quoted in Peter Hennessy, *Whitehall*, Secker & Warburg 1989, p. 683.

# Notes

6   John Guy, *Tudor England*, Oxford, Oxford University Press 1990, p. 353.

7   Professor Conrad Russell, 'Britain 1603–1990: Not Quite Federal State' Millercomm Lecture, University of Illinois, April 1990.

8   Anthony Lester, *Fundamental Rights: The United Kingdom Isolated?*, London, Sweet & Maxwell 1984, p. 65.

9   Guildhall speech, 16 November 1964.

10  Quoted in Jean-Baptiste Duroselle, *Europe: A History of its Peoples*, London, Viking 1990, p. 221.

11  Paul Kennedy, *The Realities behind Diplomacy*, London, Fontana 1981, p. 19.

12  Quoted in Paul Kennedy, *The Rise and Fall of the Great Powers*, London, Unwin Hyman 1988, p. 139.

13  A. G. L. Shaw, ed., *Great Britain and the Colonies 1815–65* London, Methuen 1970 p. 2 quoted in Paul Kennedy, *The Rise and Fall of the Great Powers*, p. 155.

14  Paul Kennedy, *The Rise and Fall of the Great Powers*, p. 158.

15  Paul Kennedy, *The Realities behind Diplomacy*, p. 318.

16  Harold Macmillan, *The Blast of War: 1939–1945*, London, Macmillan 1967, p. XV.

17  Keith Robbins, 'Insular Outsider? British History and European Integration', University of Reading Stenton Lecture 1990, p. 12: Arthur Mee, *Arthur Mee's Book of the Flag*, London, Hodder & Stoughton 1941, p. 36.

18  I am indebted to Robert Rhodes James, MP for this poem.

19  Quoted in Keith Robbins, 'Insular Outsider' p. 5.

20  Paul Kennedy, *The Rise and Fall of the Great Powers*, p. 341.

21  Correlli Barnett, *The Audit of War*, London, Macmillan 1987, p. 145.

22  David Reynolds, '1940: Fulcrum of the Twentieth Century', *International Affairs* 66 (2), 1990.

23  David Reynolds, 'A Special Relationship? America, Brit-

ain and the International Order since the Second World War', *International Affairs* 62 (1) 1985/86.

24  Christopher Tugendhat, *Making Sense of Europe*, London, Viking 1986, p. 116.

25  Martin Gilbert, *Churchill: A Life*, London, Heinemann 1991, p. 555.

26  Quoted in Hugh Thomas, *Ever Closer Union*, London, Hutchinson 1991, p. 34.

## 2  'Offshore' Attitudes

1  Theodore Zeldin, *The French*, London, Collins Harvill 1988, p. 509.

2  George Orwell, *The Lion and the Unicorn*, Harmondsworth, Penguin Books, 1982, p. 35.

3  Ibid., pp. 53–4.

4  Ibid., pp. 49–50.

5  J. E. Neale, *Queen Elizabeth I*, London, Panther 1979, pp. 306–7.

6  John Gay, *Tudor England*, Oxford, Oxford University Press, 1990, p. 359.

7  E. J. Hobsbawm, *The Age of Empire 1875–1914*, London, Cardinal 1989, p. 81.

8  I am indebted for this point to an unpublished lecture given by Professor Keith Robbins in Strasbourg.

9  Quote in J. E. Neale, *The Age of Catherine de Medici*, London, Cape 1958, p. 232.

10  Keith Robbins, *Sir Edward Grey*, Cassell 1971.

11  Selwyn Lloyd, *Suez 1956*, London, Cape 1978, p. 4.

12  Based on Gallup polls published in *The Daily Telegraph*, 12 June 1989 and *The Sunday Telegraph*, 9 December 1990.

13  *Eurobarometer*, European Community Commission, June 1990, no. 33.

14  See Peter Chippindale and Chris Horrie, *Stick It Up Your Punter!*, London, Heinemann 1990.

15 *Observer*-Harris poll, 22–23 September 1990.
16 Hugh A. MacDougall, *Racial Myth in English History*, Montreal, Harvest House 1982, p. 37.
17 Gerald Newman, *The Rise of English Nationalism*, London, Weidenfeld & Nicolson 1987.
18 Edmund Burke, *Reflections on the Revolution in France*, Harmondsworth, Penguin 1986, p. 125.
19 George Orwell, *The Lion and the Unicorn*, p. 49.
20 A. G. Macdonell, *England, their England*, London, Macmillan 1935, p. 236.
21 David Wright, 'The Fall of France', in *The War Decade* compiled by Andrew Sinclair, London, Hamish Hamilton 1989.
22 Hugo Young, *One of Us*, London, Macmillan 1989, p. 9.
23 Charles de Gaulle, *War Memoirs I – The Call to Honour*, London, Collins 1955, p. 104.
24 See John Newhouse, *De Gaulle and the Anglo-Saxons*, London, André Deutsch 1970, pp. 28–52.
25 Quoted in Stephen George, *An Awkward Partner*, Oxford, Oxford University Press 1990, p. 34.
26 Article by Patrick Marnham in *The Independent*, 21 May 1991.
27 Interview in *Le Monde*, 13 July 1989.
28 *Independent on Sunday*, 13 July 1990.
29 *Guardian*, December 1990.
30 *Observer*-Harris poll, 22–23 September 1990.
31 Paul Kennedy, *The Rise of the Anglo-German Antagonism*, London, Allen & Unwin 1980, p. 41.
32 W. Stubbs, *Constitutional History* quoted in Paul Kennedy, *The Rise of the Anglo-German Antagonism*, p. 115.
33 Paragraph based on Rosemary Ashton, *The German Idea*, Cambridge, Cambridge University Press 1980.
34 Raymond Sontag, *Germany and England 1848–1894*, New York, Appleton Century 1938, p. 121.

35  'Memorandum by Eyre Crowe', *British Documents on the Origins of the War 1898–1914*, vol, III, p. 405, London, HMSO 1928.

36  Angus Wilson, *The Strange Ride of Rudyard Kipling* London, Secker & Warburg 1978, pp. 299–300.

37  A. J. P. Taylor, *English History 1914–1945*, Oxford, Oxford University Press 1965, p. 136.

38  D. C. Watts, *Britain Looks to Germany*, London, Oswalk Wolff 1965, p. 31.

39  A. J. P. Taylor, *The Course of German History*, London, Hamish Hamilton 1951, p. 7.

40  Raymond Ebsworth, *Restoring Democracy in Germany*, London, Stevens 1960.

41  'Saying the Unsayable about the Germans', *Spectator*, 14 July 1990.

42  'What the Prime Minister Learnt about the Germans', *The Independent on Sunday*, 15 July 1990.

43  Roy Jenkins, *A Life at the Centre*, London, Macmillan 1991, p. 496.

44  Geoffrey Trease, *The Grand Tour*, London, Heinemann 1967.

45  Quoted in John Pemble, *The Mediterranean Passion*, Oxford, Oxford University Press 1988.

46  Edwin Plowden, *An Industrialist in the Treasury*, London, André Deutsch 1989, p. 93.

## 3 Perfidious Albion

1  John Milton, *The Doctrine and Discipline of Diocese*, Preface, 1644.

2  Philippe Daudy, *Les Anglais*, London, Barrie & Jenkins 1991, p. 102.

3  Quoted in Theodore Zeldin, *France 1848–1945*, vol. II Oxford, Oxford University Press 1977 p. 106.

4  Ibid., p. 103.

5  The Villiers de l'Isle Adam story is taken from Julian

# Notes

Barnes' *Flaubert's Parrot*, Picador, London 1985, pp. 41–2.

6 Hippolyte Taine, *Notes on England*, London, Strahan 1872, p. 16.

7 Jacques Bossuet, *Sermon on the Circumcision*, Metz 1652.

8 F. Holdsworth, *Joseph de Maistre et l'Angleterre*, 1935, p. 26.

9 Jean Lacouture, *De Gaulle: The Rebel 1890–1944*, London, Collins Harvill 1990, p. 220.

10 Charles de Gaulle, *Memoires de Guerre*, vol. 1, p. 70.

11 Michael Charlton, *The Price of Victory*, London, British Broadcasting Corporation, p. 262.

12 Jean Monnet, *Memoirs*, London, Collins 1978, p. 44.

13 Ibid., p. 308.

14 Ibid., p. 451.

15 *Observer*, 23 June 1991.

16 Quoted in Kennedy, *The Rise of the Anglo-German Antagonism*, p. 121.

17 Raymond Sontag, *Germany and England*, p. 325.

18 Ibid., p. 88.

19 Quoted in A. J. Marder, *From the Dreadnought to Scapa Flow*, vol. 1, Oxford, Oxford University Press 1961, p. 322.

20 Quoted in David Calleo, *The German Problem Reconsidered*, Cambridge, Cambridge University Press 1978, p. 33.

21 Quoted in Kennedy, *The Rise of the Anglo-German Antagonism*, p. 462.

22 Golo Mann, *The History of Germany since 1789*, London, Chatto & Windus 1968, p. 419.

23 Christabel Bielenberg, *The Past Is Myself*, London, Corgi 1987, pp. 145–6.

24 See Frank Giles, ed., *40 Years On: Four decades of the Königswinter Conference* published privately 1990.

25 Angelika Volle, 'Great Britain and Germany in the

199

European Community', unpublished introductory paper at 1991 Königswinter Conference.

26 Denis Mack Smith, *Cavour*, London, Methuen 1985, pp. 8, 18–19.
27 Jasper Ridley, *Garibaldi*, London, Constable 1974, p. 487.
28 Luigi Barzini, *The Europeans*, London, Penguin, pp. 39–41.
29 Iris Origo, *War in Val D'Orcia*, London, Penguin 1956, p. 12.
30 Quoted in Hugh Thomas, *Ever Closer Union*, London, Hutchinson 1991, p. 24.
31 Paul-Henri Spaak, *The Continuing Battle*, London, Weidenfeld & Nicolson 1971, pp. 76–7.
32 Roy Jenkins, *European Diary*, London, Collins 1989, p. 94.

**4 Missing European Boats**

1 Jean Monnet, *Memoirs*, London, Collins 1978, p. 314.
2 Edwin Plowden, *An Industrialist in the Treasury*, London, André Deutsch 1989, p. 72.
3 Monnet, *Memoirs* p. 293.
4 Dean Acheson, *Present at the Creation*, London, Macmillan 1970, p. 385.
5 Plowden, *Industrialist* p. 91.
6 Ibid., p. 74.
7 Denis Healey, *The Time of My Life*, London, Michael Joseph 1989, pp. 116–17.
8 Plowden, *Industrialist*, p. 94.
9 Paul-Henri Spaak, *The Continuing Battle*, London, Weidenfeld & Nicolson 1971, p. 227.
10 Ibid., p. 232.
11 Michael Charlton, *The Price of Victory*, London, British Broadcasting Corporation 1983, p. 182.
12 Ibid., p. 195.
13 Hansard, 2 August 1961.

14  Tony Benn, *Arguments for Socialism*, London, Cape 1979, p. 94.
15  Denis Healey, *Time of My Life* p. 360.
16  Roy Jenkins, *A Life at the Centre*, London, Macmillan 1991, p. 342.
17  Robert Putnam and Nicolas Bayne, *Hanging Together: The Seven Power Summits*, London, Heinemann 1984, pp. 84–5.
18  Jenkins, *A Life at the Centre*, p. 478.
19  James Callaghan, *Time and Chance*, London, Collins 1978, pp. 492–3.
20  *Britain and Europe*, London Conservative Political Centre 1988.
21  Jenkins, *A Life at the Centre*, pp. 483–5.
22  Hansard, 13 November 1990, cols 462–5.
23  Hansard, 19 November 1991, col 539.

## 5  European Destiny

1  Jean-Baptiste Duroselle, *Europe: A History of its Peoples*, London, Viking 1990, p. 413.
2  D. D. Raphael, *Adam Smith*, Oxford, Oxford University Press 1985 p. 19, quoted in William Wallace, *The Transformation of Western Europe*, London, Royal Institute of International Affairs 1990, p. 57.
3  Quoted in Theodore Besterman, *Voltaire*, London, Longmans 1969, p. 432.
4  Quoted in Jean-Baptiste Duroselle, *Europe: A History of its Peoples* p. 237.
5  See E. J. Hobsbawm, *The Age of Capital*, London, Weidenfeld and Nicolson 1975, pp. 33–34.
6  John Pinder, *Britain and the Common Market*, London, The Cresset Press 1961, p. 4.
7  Christopher Tugendhat and William Wallace, *Options for British Foreign Policy in the 1960s*, London, Chatham House Papers 1988, p. 25.

8   Alan Bullock, *Ernest Bevin 1945–1951*, London, Heinemann 1983, p. 520.

9   Christopher Tugendhat and William Wallace, *Options for British Foreign Policy in the 1960s*, p. 26.

10  Hansard, 26 June 1991, col. 1020.

11  Nicholas Ridley, *Sunday Express*, 26 August 1990; see also his *My Style of Government*, London, Hutchinson 1991, pp. 136–61.

12  Jean Monnet, *Memoirs*, London, Collins 1978, p. 450.

13  Patrick Cosgrave, *The Lives of Enoch Powell*, London, Pan 1989, p. 321.

14  Tony Benn, *Arguments for Socialism*, London, Cape 1979, p. 95.

15  George Schultz, 'On Sovereignty', lecture to the National Academy of Engineering, Washington, DC, 4 October 1989, p. 2.

16  Sir Geoffrey Howe, 'Sovereignty and Interdependence', 1990 School of Economics Alumni Lecture.

17  Quoted in Hugh Thomas, *Ever Closer Union*, London, Hutchinson 1991, p. 49.

18  William Wallace, *The Transformation of Western Europe*, p. 100.

19  Jacques Delors, *Belvedere* October/November 1991.

20  William Rees Mogg, *Independent*, 14 October 1991.

21  Hansard, 26 June 1991, col. 1035.

22  *Financial Times*, 19 October 1991.

23  *Daily Telegraph*, 5 November 1991.

24  Nicholas Colchester and David Buchan, *Europe Relaunched*, London, Hutchinson 1990, p. 164.

25  Quoted in Hugh Thomas, *Ever Closer Union*, p. 22.

26  See John Pinder, *European Community*, Oxford, Oxford University Press 1991, pp. 119–218 for a discussion of the status of the EC.

27  Paul Kennedy, *The Rise and Fall of the Great Powers*, London, Unwin Hyman 1988, pp. 472–3.

Notes

## 6 Citizens of Europe

1 Jean Monnet, *Memoirs*, London, Collins 1978, p. 308.
2 See *Eurobarometer Trends 1974–1990*, Brussels EC Commission, March 1991.
3 Robert M. Worcester, 'European Attitudes to the European Community and to 1992', *International Journal of Public Opinion Research*, vol. 2, no. 3; 'Europe Today' *The European*, 21 June 1991; *The Eurobrits*, Gallup/ GGT poll, July 1991.
4 *Daily Telegraph*, 3 August 1990; *The European*, 20 July 1990.
5 Hugh Thomas, *Ever Closer Union*, p. 24.
6 Jacques Pethmans and Alan Winter, *Europe's Domestic Market* London, Chatham House 1988, pp. 108–10.
7 *Europe 2000*, vol. II, no. 5.
8 Nicholas Colchester and David Buchan, *Europe Relaunched*, London, Hutchinson 1990, p. 7.
9 Michael Charlton, *The Price of Victory*, p. 41
10 Federico Romero, 'Cross-border Population Movements' in *The Dynamics of European Integration* William Wallace, ed., London, RIIA 1990, p. 173.
11 Alan Butt Philip, *European Border Controls: Who needs Them?*, London, RIIA 1989.
12 Christian Tyler, *Financial Times*, 1 December 1990.
13 Federico Romero, 'Cross-border Population Movements', p. 187.
14 Quoted in Michael Franklin, *Britain's Future in Europe*, London, RIIA, p. 75.
15 'Europe Today' *The European*, 21 June 1991.
16 Ibid.
17 Department of Education and Science leaflet, March 1990.
18 House of Lords Report.
19 Department of Education and Science, *The European Dimension in Education*, February 1991, p. 13.
20 *Eurobarometer*, Brussels EC Commission, December 1990, p. 67.

203

## 7 The Conversion of the Political Class?

1 Douglas Jay, *Change and Fortune*, London, Hutchinson 1980, p. 355.
2 Eric Heffer, 'Socialist Europe', *New Socialist*, no. 3, 1981.
3 The quotation is from an excellent unpublished paper 'Learning to Love the Market' by Stephen Tindale, on which some of this section is based.
4 Ibid., p. 29.
5 Denis MacShane, *French Lessons for Labour*, London, Fabian Society 1988.
6 Neil Kinnock speech to Labour Party conference, 4 October 1988.
7 Ibid.
8 Hansard, 15 November 1989, col. 390.
9 Peter Jenkins, *Independent*, 20 June 1989.
10 Nicholas Ridley, *My Style of Government*, London, Hutchinson 1991, p. 201.
11 Hansard, 13 November 1990, col. 462.
12 Hugo Young, *One of Us*, London, Macmillan 1991, p. 578.
13 Peter Jenkins, *Independent* 13 November 1991.
14 Hansard, 18 December 1991, col. 286.
15 *Independent on Sunday*, 22 December 1991.
16 *The Economist*, 11 April 1992.
17 *The Economist*, 23 November 1991.

## Conclusion: At the Heart of Europe

1 Quoted in Douglas Johnson, François Crouzet and François Bédaridon (eds.), *Britain and France: Ten Centuries*, Folkestone, Dawson, 1980, p. 16.
2 Michael Franklin, *Britain's Future in Europe*, London, Chatham House 1990, pp. 116–17.
3 Sir Leon Brittan, 'Europe: Our sort of Community', The Granada Lecture 1989, p. 5.

# Notes

4  Hansard, 26 June 1991, col. 1020.

5  Franklin, *Britain's Future in Europe*, p. 122.

6  William Wallace, 'Foreign Policy and National Identity in the United Kingdom, *International Affairs*, January 1991.

# Index

# Index

# Index

# Index

Nelson, Horatio 4, 24
Netherlands 2, 61–62, 86, 92, 94, 100, 150, 151
Newton, Isaac 65
New Zealand 93, 103
Nonsuch Treaty 1585 85
Northcliffe, Lord 25, 53
Norway 132

Observer 71–72

Ollenauer, Erich 77
Orwell, George 34–35, 44–45

Paine, Thomas 43
Palmerston, Lord 30, 60
Parker, Sir Peter 148
Peel, Robert 82
Phillip II 35, 61
Pitt, William 24
Plowden, Sir Edwin 91, 92
Poland 131, 133
Portugal 134, 150
Powell, Enoch 13, 25, 50, 128, 129
Priestley, J B 25

Radice, Evasio 82
Raleigh, Sir Walter 20
Ranke, Leopold von 52
Reagan, Ronald 29
Rhodes, Cecil 37
Ridley, Nicholas 56–57, 127, 174–175
Robertson, George 169
Rocard, Michel 167
Rome Treaty (1957) 88, 94, 102, 145, 153
Rousseau, Jean jacques 59
Ruhr 158

Ruskin, John 59
Russell, Lord John 60

Saarland 157
Sayers, Dorothy 24–25
Schengen Group 150
Schiller, Friedrich von 52
Schmidt, Helmut 29, 56, 72, 78, 80, 81, 104, 105, 135, 159
Schuman Plan 29, 62, 70, 85, 88, 90–93, 100, 109, 186
Schuman, Robert 91–93
Scotland 17, 157
Scott, Sir Walter 75
Scrivener, Christiane 137
Sedgemore, Brian 170
Seeley, J R 21
Shakespeare, William 15, 36, 65, 75–76
Shelley, Percy Bysshe 43–44
Shore, Peter 164–165
Shultz, George 129
Single European Act 84, 106–107, 130, 145, 155
Smith, Adam 82, 123
Smith, John 102, 167–168, 191–192
Smollet, Tobias 43
Soames, Christopher 47–48
Social Democrat Party (SDP) 165
Socialist International 167
Sommer, Theo 79
Soviet Union 5, 22, 126
Spaak, Paul Henri 85, 94, 95–97, 139
Spain 31, 39, 134, 139, 150, 152, 156
Spectator 56
Stauffenberg, Claus von 77

211

# Index